THE PLOT TO ATTACK IRAN

THE PLOT TO ATTACK IRAN

How the CIA and the Deep State Have Conspired to Vilify Iran

DAN KOVALIK

Skyhorse Publishing

Skyhorse Publishing books may be purchased in bulk at special discounts for sales promotion, corporate gifts, fund-raising, or educational purposes. Special editions can also be created to specifications. For details, contact the Special Sales Department, Skyhorse Publishing, 307 West 36th Street, 11th Floor, New York, NY 10018 or info@skyhorsepublishing.com.

Skyhorse® and Skyhorse Publishing® are registered trademarks of Skyhorse Publishing, Inc.®, a Delaware corporation.

Visit our website at www.skyhorsepublishing.com.

10 9 8 7 6 5 4 3 2 1

Library of Congress Cataloging-in-Publication Data is available on file.

Cover design by Michael Short

Print ISBN: 978-1-5107-3934-5
Ebook ISBN: 978-1-5107-3935-2

Printed in the United States of America

Dedicated to the people of Iran,
with love and solidarity.

Human beings are all members of one body.
They are created from the same essence.
When one member is in pain,
The others cannot rest.
If you do not care about the pain of others,
You are not worthy of being called a human.

—Sa'di, Thirteenth Century Persian Poet.
(Quote inscribed over entrance of United Nations building in NYC)*

*Phil Wilyato, *In Defense of Iran*.

CONTENTS

THE PLOT TO ATTACK IRAN

INTRODUCTION

If you're not careful, the newspapers will have you hating the people who are being oppressed, and loving the people who are doing the oppressing.
—Malcolm X

I VISITED IRAN FOR THE FIRST time in July of 2017. Indeed, quite ironically, I was in Iran for the Fourth of July. And, while there were no fireworks on that day to commemorate US Independence Day, I assure the reader that I felt absolutely no antipathy from the Iranian people, despite my being a citizen of the nation which has been referred to by some Iranians as the Great Satan. Rather, as I'm sure nearly every American tourist in Iran can tell you, the Iranians have a special affection for Americans, and when strangers on the street found out I was from the United States, they would invariably smile, welcome me to their country, show off their English if they were able to speak it, and enthusiastically pose for a photo-op.

Like most people in the world, the people of Iran quite readily, and maturely, distinguish individual Americans from their government—a government which many Iranians do have a problem with, and for very good reason.

Iran is actually a quite modern country with many Western influences. Many people I met spoke some English, some quite fluently, and most signs were in both Farsi and English. And, while nearly every woman wore some type of head covering—a legal requirement in Iran, though enforcement of the requirement has been relaxed by the police in Tehran as of late—very few wear a burka which covers their face.

Instead, most women (some of the most beautiful I have seen anywhere) wear light, colorful silk scarves around their heads, while wearing very modern clothes otherwise, including, for example, blue jeans and high heels. Actually, I found it quite amusing that nearly no women wore head coverings at all on the flight from Frankfurt, Germany, but when the pilot announced our initial descent into Tehran, nearly all the women put on their scarves in unison.

I think it is quite fair to say that women indeed fare better in Iran than in nearly any other country in the Middle East, and in many ways better than before the 1979 Islamic Revolution. Thus, literacy for women is now over 80 percent while it was around 25 percent in 1970; 90 percent of women are enrolled in school, which is free for all even through university; while about one-third of university students were women before 1979, now women make up a strong majority (65 to 70 percent) of university students; and women participate in every field of economic and social life, including sports, film, police, medicine, science, business, and entertainment.[1]

Women actually do better in Iran than in the United States in a few key ways—for example, they are legally entitled to ninety days maternity leave at two-thirds pay,[2] whereas in the United States they have no entitlement to maternity leave at all. Iran has an equal pay for equal work requirement,[3] a measure which the United States does not have and indeed has opposed vigorously, most notably by refusing to ratify international human rights instruments which require this, especially the Convention on the Elimination of All Forms of Discrimination against Women (CEDAW). It must be noted that the United States and Iran share the distinction of being among the few countries which are not parties to CEDAW, the others being Palau, The Holy See, Somalia, Sudan, and Tonga.

Iranian women have an entitlement to employer-provided child care centers whereas, again, they have no such right in the United States.[4]

Some other fun facts are that Iran is one of the only countries in the world that requires couples to take a class on modern contraception before being issued a marriage license. Iran also has the only state-sponsored condom factory in the Middle East—the Keyhan Bod plant—which produces seventy million condoms a year in various colors and flavors.[5] In addition, there are more sex change operations in Iran than any country in the world besides Thailand.[6] Since 2005, when the much-maligned Ahmadinejad was president, the government has been providing grants of up to $4,500 for the operation, plus further funding for hormone therapy.[7]

Meanwhile, the one big downside for me, a guy who enjoys a glass or two of red wine in the evening, is that alcohol is illegal in Iran. And so, while the airport and hotel we stayed at (the former Tehran Hyatt) had bars, they did not serve alcohol; only juice, coffee, and tea.

In addition, the airport, hotel, and nearly every building we visited were adorned with giant framed photos of both the infamous Ayatollah Khomeini, who I was taught to hate and fear as a child, and the current Supreme Leader, Ayatollah Khamenei, who certainly has a softer, kinder look than his predecessor. I desperately wanted to take a selfie in front of these pictures, but, for fear of offending someone, I never did.

I have read that, notwithstanding Iran's dry law, many Iranians have a private stock of liquor, and that Iranians indeed compete very well with other nations, Russia included, for alcohol consumption. I sat next to a German petro-engineer on the plane to Tehran. He told me that he often comes to Iran for work, and that he has gotten to know some Iranians very well. He explained how he was at an Iranian family's home one evening for dinner, and they asked him how he liked their food. He responded, "It is wonderful, but I am from Germany; it would go down much better with a glass of beer." And then, from seemingly out of nowhere, bottles of Heineken and other spirits appeared on the table. Apparently, this is a typical happening, but not knowing anyone very well in Iran, I did not have such an experience.

Even stone cold sober, however, I loved Iran. The people are friendly and famously hospitable. Indeed, I was almost embarrassed by the hospitality. My hosts, from the University of Tehran which had invited several of us from the States to speak there, were constantly making sure that we had enough to eat and drink, and that we always had a place to rest, even in the middle of the day. The Iranians that accompanied us would often disappear themselves in the early afternoon, and we later learned that they were going to the nearest prayer room—not to pray, however, but to sleep on the floor.

Iranians would consider it an act of barbarity to make us take a cab to or from the airport, as opposed to being personally driven. In contrast, I can't remember the last time someone personally took me or picked me up at the airport back home in Pittsburgh.

At the mosques, moreover, it was quite common for people to give visitors, such as myself, offerings of food, such as homemade candies. At the first mosque we visited in Tehran—the Imamzadeh-Saleh Mosque—our guide pointed out the burial places of four of the nuclear scientists assassinated by Israel, quite possibly with the help of the terrorist group known as the MEK. These scientists are considered martyrs, a very big honor in the Shia religious tradition.

Of course, there are many dazzling and breathtaking antiquities to gaze at in Iran. I was very fortunate because the University of Tehran generously offered to fly a couple of us to the ancient city of Esfahan (also spelled "Isfahan") which is a one-hour flight south of Tehran.

In Esfahan, we spent a day walking through the Imam Square (also known as Meidan Emam or Naghsh-e Jahan), truly a sight to behold. Imam Square is one of over twenty UNESCO-designated world heritage sites in Iran. This is UNESCO's description of the Square:

> The Meidan Emam is a public urban square in the centre of Esfahan,
> a city located on the main north-south and east-west routes crossing

central Iran. It is one of the largest city squares in the world and an outstanding example of Iranian and Islamic architecture. Built by the Safavid shah Abbas I in the early 17th century, the square is bordered by two-storey arcades and anchored on each side by four magnificent buildings: to the east, the Sheikh Lotfallah Mosque; to the west, the pavilion of Ali Qapu; to the north, the portico of Qeyssariyeh; and to the south, the celebrated Royal Mosque. A homogenous urban ensemble built according to a unique, coherent, and harmonious plan, the Meidan Emam was the heart of the Safavid capital and is an exceptional urban realization.

Also known as Naghsh-e Jahan ("Image of the World"), and formerly as Meidan-e Shah, Meidan Emam is not typical of urban ensembles in Iran, where cities are usually tightly laid out without sizeable open spaces. Esfahan's public square, by contrast, is immense: 560 m long by 160 m wide, it covers almost 9 ha [i.e., 24.3 acres]. All of the architectural elements that delineate the square, including its arcades of shops, are aesthetically remarkable, adorned with a profusion of enameled ceramic tiles and paintings.[8]

Sadly, as UNESCO laments, the Imam Square is being threatened by the most relentless of forces—time—and Iran's inability to keep up maintenance of the ancient structures. The Western sanctions against Iran only curtail Iran's ability to maintain such treasures. However, I did notice while in Esfahan that at least some of the buildings were covered with scaffolding and under repair.

As I witnessed, this Square is teeming with activity, with people picnicking, playing music, shopping, or sitting to enjoy some ice cream on what is almost invariably a hot, sunny day. I myself spent the day in the Square taking numerous photos, particularly of the people there, and they seemed excited about how much I appreciated them and their country.

When one is in Esfahan, one must visit the amazing bazaars which help to form Imam Square, and we of course did just that. While I was at one of the bazaars, I was invited to drink espresso in a Persian car- pet dealer's store while the ring I was buying as a souvenir (a silver ring with a black opal and with the word "Ali" in Farsi carved beauti- fully into both sides) was being fitted for me by the vendor's son.

The vendor, known as a bazaari, immediately started taking out rugs, unrolling them, and telling us of the history of each one. Some of the rugs, though they looked brand new, were a hundred years old or more. The craftsmanship put into these, probably the most famous type of rug in the world, is awe-inspiring. In the end, the bazaari's hospitality paid off, as my American companion bought a rug from him, and I purchased an incredible backpack which looked like it was made from a Persian rug.

This bazaari, I must note, was the only one I met in Iran who could process a credit card. Somehow, he managed to have cards processed through Dubai. Because of the Western sanctions against Iran, US credit and ATM cards do not otherwise work in Iran, making a tourist trip to that country quite challenging for an American.

Another interesting consequence of the Western isolation of Iran is that international copyright and trademark laws are not honored there. And so, for example, there were a number of knock-off busi- nesses which passed themselves off as American chains, such as Starbucks and Kentucky Fried Chicken, though they usually were named just slightly differently. The KFC I saw, complete with a picture of Colonel Sanders, was named ZFC, though no one could tell me what the "Z" stands for.

While in Esfahan, we also visited the famous Monar Jonban, liter- ally, "Shaking Minarets," a monument built in the 1300s to cover the grave of Amu Abdollah Soqla, a Muslim hermit. The monument's two tall minarets are spring-loaded and built to shake so that they can withstand an earthquake. Several times a day, the minarets are shaken manually to the sound of music as bystanders look on and applaud.

Iran, and Esfahan in particular, while known primarily for their spectacular Islamic architecture, also have amazing architecture from other religions and cultures. For example, there are a number of beautiful Armenian Christian churches—one that I visited in Esfahan is still a functioning place of worship and has an exhibit memorializing the Armenian genocide. I was also able to visit the ancient Zoroastrian Fire Temple, Atashgah, which looks like a giant sand castle on a hill.

And, one might be surprised to hear that I also visited a functioning synagogue in Esfahan (once called "Dar-Al-Yahud," or, "House of the Jews"). I went looking for the synagogue after seeing a shopkeeper in a bazaar wearing a yarmulke. Iran is actually home to twenty-five thousand Jews—the second largest Jewish population in the Middle East outside of Israel. And, in addition to synagogues, Esfahan is also home to a two-thousand-year-old Jewish cemetery as well as Jewish mausoleums.

Iranians are indeed proud of the fact that the famous Persian Emperor in Persepolis, Cyrus the Great, upon conquering Babylon, "freed the Jews who had been held there in slavery, returned them to Jerusalem and gave them resources to rebuild their temple."[9]

The director of Tehran's Jewish Committee, Siamak Morsadegh, recently gave an interview in which he described the experience of Jews in modern Iran, and dispelled a number of myths about Iran in the process:[10]

It's a lot better than many people think. Jews are a recognized minority here, so we can practice our religion freely. We have more than 20 working synagogues in Tehran and at least five kosher butcheries. In some European countries that is not allowed because of animal rights. In Iran, it is.

Generally speaking, the Jews' condition in Iran has always been better than in Europe. In our country's history, there was never a time when all Iranians had the same religion, race or language, so there is a high degree of tolerance. Jews and Muslims respect each other, but at the same time, we know there are differences.

The hospital I work in is a Jewish hospital, for example, but more than 95 percent of both our personnel and patients is Muslim. It's strictly forbidden to ask about religion there because the most important verse of Torah, which is written on top of the hospital, says: "Treat other people like yourself." It does not say "other Jews," it says "other people." It shows that we have a practical relationship with each other and cooperate to make the world a better place.

But I am Iranian—I pray in Hebrew and I can speak in English, but I can only think in Persian. In my opinion there is a big difference between nationality and religion; they are not in opposition to each other. Going abroad—and especially going to Israel—is not an option for me, because I think the idea that Jews have to live in one special place in the world is rooted in the idea that we are different from other people. But I think we are equal.

In the same interview, Siamak Morsadegh addressed head-on some of the inflammatory statements made by Iranian President Ahmadinejad about the Holocaust and Israel:

We did not agree with President Ahmadinejad, and we told him so. He did not directly deny the Holocaust, he questioned it—but I do not even accept questioning it. It doesn't make sense to question things that are completely clear and accepted all around the world.

But that did not disturb our day-to-day life. The financial help for our Jewish hospital by the government, for example, started during Ahmadinejad's presidency. He was anti-Israel, not anti-Semitic. Iran's general policy is not changed by its presidents anyway. The main policymaker is Supreme Leader [Ayatollah Ali Khamenei], and the main framework is the constitution.

These are not mere idle words, either, for the proof is in the pudding. As journalist Jonathan Cook explains, the relative success of Jews in Iran "and their repeated refusal to leave, despite financial incentives offered by Israel and American Jewish groups for them to emigrate, have proved an enduring embarrassment to those claiming that the Iranian regime is driven by genocidal anti-Semitism."[11]

In truth, Iran is proud of the pluralistic nature of its society and its tolerance of many faiths. Indeed, as the United States has itself recognized for a long time, as evidenced in a December 27, 1978, Confidential Country Team Report drafted by the US Embassy in Tehran: "The Shi'a sect of Islam predominates in Iran but the country has had a long history of religious toleration which has allowed such religious minorities as Christians, Jews, Zoroastrians and members of the Baha'i sect to practice their beliefs openly and to participate fully in public life."[12]

One might be surprised to learn that, to this very day, the biggest holiday in Iran is not in fact Islamic but is indeed the three-thousand-year-old Zoroastrian New Year's Day celebration known as Nowruz (New Day).[13] Iran as a nation existed, in fact, for over two millennia before Islam ever came into being.[14] And, Iran's language, Farsi, is more like French and Swedish than Arabic, the Iranian people being distinctly and proudly non-Arabs.[15]

I often thought to myself during my stay in Iran that, despite Iran being invaded multiple times over its long history, including by the Mongols who actually left much of the architecture intact, the ancient buildings I gazed at were still there because the United States had yet to invade it. The other countries in the region that have been "graced" by the US military in recent years, such as Iraq, Afghanistan, and Libya, now lay in ruins, possibly never to be rebuilt again.

As one example, just this morning, I heard an NPR story about Mosul, Iraq, where the United States finished a very brutal operation over seven months ago. They interviewed an Iraqi who complained that he still cannot return to his home because it still contains the bones of the ISIS fighters killed in the battle, that the roads have yet to be cleared, and the 150,000 homes or so destroyed in the battle have yet to be rebuilt.[16]

NPR quoted former Secretary of State Rex Tillerson, who just shrugged it off by saying that the United States—which had opened up Pandora's Box in Iraq to begin with by its 2003 invasion—does not engage in nation-building anymore (if it ever really did), and that the Gulf countries should help with the rebuilding.[17] Commenting on this, Jeffrey St. Claire of *CounterPunch* quipped, "So much for the Pottery Barn Rule. It's back to the Tacitus Rule: 'We made wasteland and called it peace.'"[18]

Meanwhile, many Iranians mistook me for being Persian before I opened my mouth and spoke English, and they seemed overjoyed to meet an American who looked like them. My new friend Ali (it seemed to me that nearly every man in Iran is named either Ali or Moham-mad), a young man who served as our interpreter, was quite amused by this. Ali is both a die-hard supporter of the Islamic Republic as well as one of the sweetest people I've ever met. He turned to me once, cupping my face in his hands, and said, "You have such a kind face; you look like the men who volunteered to fight against Saddam Hussein."

Ali was referring, of course, to the brutal war between Iran and Iraq in which thousands of Iranian volunteers (the Baseeji, or Popular Mobilization Army) went to the front lines to supplement the fledging revolutionary military and to confront the Iraqi invaders with "human wave" attacks.[19] These "human wave" attacks were quite successful until Iraq came up with the brilliant plan to counter them with chemical weapons, of course bought from Germany and the United States.

Saddam Hussein preemptively launched this war, with great encouragement from the United States and the rest of the West, to try to overturn the Islamic government which had just come to power and to annex land from Iran given up in the 1975 Algiers Agreement. The war, known then as the Gulf War until the United States appropriated that name for its 1991 invasion of Iraq,[20] lasted from 1980 to 1988, with the United States at times, and quite cynically, supporting both sides of the armed conflict.

On the first evening of our visit to Esfahan, Ali accompanied us across one of the eleven spectacular stone bridges that, at that moment, crossed the completely dry Zayandeh River. Five of the eleven bridges, including the one we crossed, are over four hundred years old. When there is a big rain, the bank then fills up with the Zayandeh. Sadly, Iran these days is frequently battling drought, so we never witnessed this. However, we did hear the frogs, at least a reminder of the river, croaking at the moonlight.

These bridges are truly a sight to behold. The one we crossed is called the Si-o-Seh Bridge, built in 1602, and is known as the "Bridge of 33 Arches." These arches are lit up yellowish orange at night. The glow from the arches is quite magical. People of all ages, including babies being pushed in strollers, traverse these bridges into the wee hours. As Ali noted, "It is safe here. Even women can go out alone at night without worry."

Ali was so proud to show me his country, including the Revolutionary Guard who manned the security at the airport. A devotee of American cinema, Ali said, as we approached security, "You will see the Revolutionary Guard with their green uniforms and thick beards just as the ones depicted in the movie *Argo*" (the film about the American hostage-taking which won Best Picture at the Academy Awards), "but you will see that they are very nice."

I asked Ali how he liked the movie *Argo*, which obviously depicts the Americans as the good guys. He said, with a smile on his face, "I hated it, of course; I am Iranian."

* * *

While at age eleven I was not aware of the February 1979 Islamic Revolution which overthrew the Shah of Iran, I was quite aware, as anyone my age and older, of the taking of the American hostages in the US Embassy in Tehran which followed soon thereafter and which lasted for 444 days. I remember the rage we as Americans collectively felt as we saw the tally of the days these hostages were held tick upwards every evening on the nightly news. And, our rage was focused on the personification of the revolutionary government of Iran at that time—the Ayatollah Khomeini—who was also portrayed as the personification of evil itself.

I also recall vividly the failed attempt by Jimmy Carter to rescue the hostages, and then the joy I felt when the hostages were finally released within mere minutes of Ronald Reagan's inauguration as President. Growing up in a firmly Republican household, I believed that this series of events demonstrated the incompetence and weakness of Carter on the one hand, and the omnipotence of Reagan on the other, as the mere swearing-in of the tough-talking and resolute Reagan appeared to have frightened the Iranians into releasing the hostages.

The vilification of Khomeini and Iran was, and continues to be, made easy by the omission of many salient facts in the prevailing, and quite one-sided, narrative of the US-Iranian saga. And, the story of the apparent incompetence of Carter versus the apparent superhero quality of Reagan also unravels upon close inspection of facts which are rarely discussed in polite company, if known at all.

Such things are never taught in high school, and certainly not mine, a Catholic school in Cincinnati whose powerhouse football team (on which I played) was dubbed "The Holy Crusaders," after the Christian knights sent to invade, conquer, and pillage the Muslim world in the name of Jesus Christ.

I only became aware of such facts in college, and even then, not in any classroom. Rather, I learned of such things, which I discuss in this book, when my college friends and I began delving into the crimes of the CIA and US imperialism. I then became aware that Iran has been more of the victim of unjust US policies than the other way around, and that the fear and rage some Iranians expressed in the hostage-taking was rooted in very real grievances growing out of the US-backed coup against their democratically-elected prime minister in 1953, the United States' installing of the murderous Shah (or king) in his stead, and the United States' support for the Shah and his torture state until the bitter end which only came about in 1979 with the Islamic Revolution.

And, the twisted nature of the US-Iranian relationship did not end there. Indeed, what none of the US public knew at the time the hostages were being held, and which few even know today, is that Reagan, far from playing the hero in this story, acted the part of a conniving villain. Indeed, Reagan, with the help of the CIA and Israel's Mossad, went behind Jimmy Carter's back and derailed his efforts to free the hostages in order to greatly improve his chances of becoming president. And, the seemingly miraculous timing of the freeing of the hostages within five minutes of Reagan's inauguration turned out to be the product, not of Reagan's greatness, but of his dirty deal with the hostage-takers to hold the hostages until after he was safely in office. In a very real way, then, Reagan himself became the captor of these hostages in their final months of captivity.

Reagan would then go on to encourage Saddam Hussein, then the United States' close friend, to lead Iraq into invading Iran in 1980 in order to try to overturn the Iranian Revolution. This deadly war, which lasted until 1988, resulted in the deaths of around one million people, and included Saddam's gassing of Iranians, and Kurds as well, with US knowledge and acquiescence. To make matters even worse, Reagan at one point helped arm Iran during the war, even as he was aiding Iraq, in order to obtain needed cash to fund the Nicaraguan Contras— a terrorist group which Congress had stopped funding because of their abysmal human rights record—and in order to weaken both Iran and Iraq as powers in the Middle East.

Once I learned this tragic history, I lost all of the antipathy I felt towards Iran as a child. Instead, I felt only love and empathy for the people of Iran who I came to understand have suffered much more at our hands than we at theirs. And, watching the United States go from one destructive war to the next, invariably justifying each war on the basis of claims which quickly turned out to be lies, I decided that I could not stand silently by as the United States stumbled into another war with a beautiful country which not only deserves our respect, but which deserves a long-awaited apology for what our nation has done to it and its people.

1

TARGET: IRAN

We're going to take out seven countries in five years, starting with Iraq, and then Syria, Lebanon, Libya, Somalia, Sudan and, finishing off, Iran.
—US General Wesley Clark, former Supreme Commander of NATO[1]

THE DRUMS OF WAR ARE BEATING yet again. As they often have for the past thirty-plus years, they are beating in this country for a war with Iran. I have written this book in an attempt to stop such a war—a war which I believe would not only be unjust, illegal, and immoral, but which would be truly devastating for both Iran and the United States, and, indeed, for the entire world.

By many accounts, the United States, and its close ally Israel, have been preparing for a war with Iran for well over a decade now. As veteran journalists such as Seymour Hersh and Jonathan Cook have documented, the Bush Administration was keen on a military attack against Iran in 2005.[2] It appears that Bush began concrete preparations for such an attack in 2006. According to Seymour Hersh, by the spring of 2006, the White House had increased clandestine activities inside Iran and intensified planning for a possible major air attack. Current and former American military and intelligence officials said that Air Force planning groups are drawing up lists of targets, and teams of American combat troops have been ordered into Iran, under cover, to collect targeting data and to establish contact with anti-government ethnic-minority groups.[3]

Plans were even being made for tactical nuclear weapons strikes against various targets in Iran.

According to such accounts, Israel's 2006 assault upon Hezbollah in Southern Lebanon was the opening salvo against Iran (Hezbollah being a critical ally of Iran in striking distance of Israel).

However, the strong resistance which Hezbollah put up against Israel's four-week assault, combined with the equally strong resistance of the Iraqi people after the 2003 invasion—an invasion which Secretary of State Donald Rumsfeld promised would end quickly with a modest military force—necessitated a delay in an attack upon Iran. However, the goal for such an attack has never been removed from the table.

Indeed, while many viewed President Obama's 2015 "nuclear deal" with Iran as a move towards peace with that country, there are good arguments for the proposition that this deal (formally known as the Joint Comprehensive Plan of Action, or JCPOA) was always a Trojan Horse. And so, when President Trump stated that this deal was the "worst ever," he was right, though not in the way he meant—in reality, it was the "worst ever" for Iran, and was always intended to be so.

The general outline of the nuclear deal was that, in return for the lifting of UN sanctions which were ostensibly imposed in response to Iran's nuclear enrichment program, Iran would give up this program. Iran was desperate for the lifting of these sanctions, which severely undermined its economy, and which made further investment in much-needed social programs impossible. For its part, the United States claimed it wanted the deal to end any attempt by Iran to build nuclear weapons, though the United States' own National Intelligence Estimate concluded that Iran did not have such intention, and in any case was years away from having nuclear weapons capability.

At the same time, as learned the hard way by Libya, which had given up its nuclear ambitions to placate the West only to be invaded shortly thereafter, and as proven by North Korea whose nukes brought Trump to the bargaining table, the only way a weaker state can protect itself against the United States is to have a nuclear deterrent. Indeed, as Israel's leading military historian, Martin Van Creveld, has opined, Iran would be insane if it were not trying to develop nuclear weapons. Thus, according to Creveld:

> Even if the Iranians are working on a bomb, Israel may not be their real concern. Iran is now surrounded by American forces on all sides—in the Central Asian republics to the north, Afghanistan to the east, the Gulf to the south and Iraq to the West . . . Wherever U.S. forces go, nuclear weapons go with them or can be made to follow in short order. The world has witnessed how the United States attacked Iraq for, as it turned out, no reason at all. Had the Iranians not tried to build nuclear weapons, they would be crazy.[4]

Iran, not so much crazy, but desperate for the end of sanctions, agreed to give up its nuclear ambitions, even those related to pressing energy concerns.

The United States, however, was motivated to end Iran's nuclear ambitions for the precise purpose of leaving Iran vulnerable to attack, just as Creveld explained it would be without a nuclear deterrent. But there was another way in which the nuclear deal would set Iran up for invasion, one which is not so apparent.

As geopolitical researcher Tony Cartalucci explains, the bad faith of the United States in signing the nuclear deal is evidenced by its actions in engaging in proxy wars against Iran—in Syria, Lebanon, and in Iran itself through terrorist groups—even as it was signing on the dotted line.[5] Cartalucci writes that, "[a]ccording to years of US policy papers, dismantling Iran's allies in Syria and Lebanon were crucial prerequisites toward eventually undermining and overthrowing the government and political order in Iran itself."

But there is even further proof of the United States' duplicity beyond this—the words of a key policy paper written years before the United States entered into the nuclear deal. As Cartalucci relates,

> Beyond US policymakers openly conspiring to weaken or altogether dismantle Iran's regional allies before setting upon Iran directly, years before the JCPOA was signed, US policymakers pledged to propose then intentionally betray a "superb offer" to help portray Iran rather than the United States as both an irrational threat to global security and a nation bent on acquiring nuclear weapons for the "wrong reasons."

The 2009 Brookings Institution report "Which Path to Persia?" explicitly described this ploy, stating:

> . . . any military operation against Iran will likely be very unpopular around the world and require the proper international context—both to ensure the logistical support the operation would require and to minimize the blowback from it. The best way to minimize international opprobrium and maximize support (however grudging or covert) is to strike only when there is a widespread conviction that the Iranians were given but then rejected a superb offer—one so good that only a regime determined to acquire nuclear weapons and acquire them for the wrong reasons would turn it down. Under those circumstances, the United States (or Israel) could portray its operations as taken in sorrow, not anger, and at least some in the international community would conclude that the Iranians "brought it on themselves" by refusing a very good deal.[6] (emphasis in original)

Cartalucci further relates that "shortly before US President Barack Obama ended his second term in office, preparations were already underway to backtrack on the Iran deal. With US President Donald Trump now presiding over US foreign policy, the US is preparing to either entirely withdraw from the deal or rewrite its conditions in such a fashion that Iran will be unable to accept it."

In other words, Trump's current threats to undo the nuclear deal—threats which many properly view as a prelude to war—can be seen as a continuation of Obama's plans against Iran, just as Obama's plans were a continuation of Bush's. Indeed, while few in this country are willing to admit it, there is an undeniable continuity in the foreign policy practices of US presidents, whether they be Republicans or Democrats.

Quite possibly, this is because there are greater forces at work than our elected officials, such as the military industrial complex that President Eisenhower warned us of back in the 1950s, which defines our nation's international trajectory. And, as we shall see, the United States' treachery against Iran can indeed be traced as far back as the Eisenhower Administration.

As I learned while in Iran, the current Supreme Leader of Iran, Ayatollah Ali Khamenei, was always against negotiating with Obama over the nuclear deal, believing that the United States is not a reliable bargaining partner. Of course, the Ayatollah had good reason to doubt the United States' sincerity in bargaining, given that its track record has been pretty bad, even hearkening back in colonial times when European settlers in the New World made deals with the Native Americans which they then turned around and reneged on even before the ink on the deal was dry.

And, in the classic US tradition of projecting our own worst characteristics upon others, the settlers added insult to injury by referring to those who do not keep their word as "Indian givers,"[7] when in fact they should be called "Settler givers" or "White givers." This type of projection is also seen in the United States' current accusations against others, such as Iran itself, as being state sponsors of terrorism when, as we shall shortly see, it is the United States which is the greatest sponsor of terror in the world.

Of course, a more apt example of such "Settler giving" was Obama's dealings with Libya's Muammar Gaddafi, prevailing upon Gaddafi to give up Libya's nuclear ambitions and seemingly welcoming Gaddafi back into the community of nations, only to invade his country, topple his government, and aid and abet Gaddafi's brutal murder a short time thereafter.

In any case, because the Iranian president, Hassan Rouhani, wanted the deal so badly to be able to make good on massive social spending he had promised Iranians, Khamenei told him to go ahead with talks. In the end, Khamenei, in his substantial wisdom, was correct in his misgivings. But given the potential tragic consequences of being proven right, there is little for Khamenei to gloat about.

2

THE WEST'S NOT-SO-CREATIVE DESTRUCTION OF THE MIDDLE EAST

Creative destruction is our middle name, both within our society and
abroad. We tear down the old order every day, from business to science,
literature, art, architecture, and cinema to politics and the law.
Our enemies have always hated this whirlwind of energy and creativity,
which menaces their traditions (whatever they may be) and shames them
for the inability to keep pace. Seeing America undo traditional
societies, they fear us, for they do not wish to be undone. . . .
We must destroy them to advance our historic mission.
—Michael Ledeen, US Neo-Con[1]

UNLIKE MANY IN THIS COUNTRY, I simply do not view Iran as a menace—neither to its neighbors, nor as a threat to us in any way. To the contrary, I see Iran as a country which is itself under existential threat and with much to fear, and Iran surely sees itself as a country under attack from all sides. One need only look at a map to see why this is so.

Iran, known as Persia until WWII, is a country about the size of Alaska, and with about eighty million people. It borders many nations, nearly all of which it views to be hostile. It is bordered by Iraq, Turkey, Afghanistan, Turkmenistan, Armenia, Azerbaijan, Pakistan, the Caspian Sea to the north, and the Persian Gulf to the south, with Saudi Arabia, Kuwait, Bahrain, United Arab Emirates, Qatar, and Oman lying just across the Persian Gulf.

And, unlike most of its neighbors which have changed their identity and borders numerous times—or, more to the point, have had their borders changed for them—Iran has, despite being invaded on many occasions, remained a single, unified nation since 2500 BCE. As a consequence, Iran is "one of the more socially cohesive societies in the Middle East."[2]

For his part, writer Stephen Kinzer explains:

Many countries in the Middle East are artificial creations. European colonialists drew their national borders in the nineteenth or twentieth century, often with little regard for local history and tradition, and their leaders have had to concoct outlandish myths in order to give citizens a sense of nationhood. Just the opposite is true of Iran. This is one of the world's oldest nations, heir to a tradition that reaches back thousands of years, to periods when great conquerors extended their rule across continents, poets and artists created works of exquisite beauty, and one of the world's extraordinary religious traditions took root and flowered.[3]

Sadly, Iran's ancient and proud history is often forgotten, or intentionally disregarded by the great powers, which have seen Iran only for its geo-political importance and its greatest resource—oil. During the Cold War, for example, when Iran bordered the southern part of the Soviet Union, it was viewed, especially by US foreign policy leaders, as a key chess piece in the struggle between the United States and the USSR.

With the collapse of the Soviet Union in 1991, and the consequent weakening of Russia as a world power, the United States has been committed to maintaining a unipolar world in which it is the one superpower. This doctrine was best expressed by President George H.W. Bush in his January 29, 1991, State of the Union Address in which he famously announced the construction of a "New World Order" which would be led by the United States—a nation he and other US presidents (e.g., Obama in his parting words to Trump) described as "indispensable." Bush stated, "The United States bears a major share of leadership in this effort. Among the nations of the world, only the United States of America has both the moral standing and the means to back it up. We're the only nation on this Earth that could assemble the forces of peace. This is the burden of leadership and the strength that has made America the beacon of freedom in a searching world."[4]

As author and political commentator Stephen Gowans explains,

> The implication of Bush's New World Order was that the planet would be divided between nations destined to be dominated and one nation, the United States, which would dominate. Only the United States would have the right to independence, and the Pentagon, CIA, and US state and treasury departments would exercise leadership over the affairs of other countries. The expression of Bush's declaration of US world leadership can be seen in the words of a Pentagon spokesman, Rear Admiral John Kirby, who, in 2015, declared that the United States retains the "right," the "responsibility," and "the resources" to intervene in any country unilaterally to achieve US foreign policy goals.[5]

The announcement of this "New World Order," combined with the United States' first invasion of Iraq in 1990-1991, changed Iran's perception of its security in its region of the world and its relationship with Israel, which had been largely cooperative up to that point, despite the rhetoric of both countries against the other.[6] In short, Iran decided that it had to aggressively protect its existence and interests in the Middle East in light of what it reasonably saw as the US-Israeli goal of remaking the region.[7] As we would see time and time again, the United States' own actions would unnecessarily provoke Iran and turn a potential and willing friend into an adversary.

In addition, with Russia's demise as a world power and Iraq's demise as a regional power after successive US invasions, Iran has emerged once more as a regional power of its own—a power which the United States and the West are obsessed with containing as a threat to the "New World Order." And the United States in particular has used ever more desperate and devilish means to try to do this.

Meanwhile, it is Iran's unbroken history and powerful traditions which make it the great nation it is, and which makes it so important to the Middle East and to all of humanity. Indeed, Iran is a critical civilizing influence in the world, if for no other reason than that it is intent upon preserving the culture and history within its borders and within its region of the world—a region which is indeed known as the "cradle of civilization," having given birth to Christianity, Judaism, Islam, and agriculture.

The United States, on the other hand, though seeing itself as the protector of civilization, is destroying this region of the world, seemingly with intent. As just one example, Iran watched in 2003 as its neighbor Iraq—through which run both the Tigris and Euphrates rivers and thus where the Garden of Eden might have been—was invaded by the United States and its coalition partners, suffering the worst destruction it ever had since the Mongol invasion of 1258 led by Genghis Khan. And Iranians are painfully aware that the United States is intent on doing the very same to their country.

The United States has made it clear, certainly since President George W. Bush named Iran as part of the "Axis of Evil" in his 2002 State of the Union Address, that it is intent on militarily attacking Iran. In the meantime, the United States has been trying to weaken Iran through a combination of diplomatic isolation, economic warfare, sanctions, support for anti-government groups in Iran, and support of terrorism in nearby countries and in Iran itself.

And so, beginning in late 2017, there were substantial anti-government demonstrations in Iran, which President Trump immediately seized upon as a sign that the people of Iran were ready to overthrow their government in the interest of freedom, and Trump and others certainly encouraged them to do so. Never mind that in a recent poll by the Center for International and Security Studies at Maryland only 0.3 percent of Iranians ranked "lack of civil liberties" in their country as their number one concern, whereas 40.1 percent listed unemployment, 12.5 percent listed inflation and high cost of living, 9.4 percent listed youth umemployment, and 6.9 percent listed low incomes.[8]

In other words, by far the biggest concern Iranians have is with their economy, and, to the extent the US press was honest about this fact, nearly none explained how the West is largely behind Iran's economic woes.

One source which discussed this was the *Independent* of London, which, in an August 9, 2017, article explained how in early 2014 "Saudi Arabia launched this oil price war in tandem with the U.S.," with the "main goal of crushing Russian and Iranian power and influence."[9] The story goes on to explain, by the way, how Venezuela became collateral damage of this war, much to the joy of the United States, of course.

As the *Independent* relates, Saudi Arabia ran this play successfully against Iran in the late 1970s. Thus, "Back in 1977, when Iran was planning extensive nuclear power plants [by the way, with the approval and support of the United States] and envisaging the spread of its influence throughout the Middle East, the Saudi regime swamped the markets, expanding oil production from 8 million to almost 12 million barrels a day, sharply cutting the oil prices. Iran watched billions of dollars in anticipated oil revenues vanish, and the Shah was forced to abandon his plans for nuclear investment. Manufacturing collapsed, inflation skyrocketed, unemployment rose steeply—and before long economic troubles had destroyed all support for the Iranian monarchy."

While the *Independent* does not go into this, it must be said that the United States supported Saudi Arabia's oil war in 1977 for the same reason it supports it today—to undermine Russia, back then the USSR, of course. And, this oil war would help to fatally undermine the USSR as well.

The *Independent* explains how Saudi Arabia pushed world oil production from a steady eighty million barrels a day to around ninety-seven million barrels by late 2015 in a repeat of its war against Iran.

With the current US economic sanctions added to this oil war, Iran and its people have suffered greatly and will continue to, but this is all according to plan, with the hope being that the people will suffer enough to support another regime change. Yes, this is a cruel policy—indeed an act of economic terrorism in that it constitutes the intentional infliction of injury against the civilian population to bring about a desired political end—but it is par for the course for the United States. And, as we shall see, the United States ran this play quite successfully in toppling Iran's first democratic leader in the 1950s.

Commentator Vijay Prashad is one of the few journalists to link US sanctions and the US-Saudi oil war to the recent protests in Iran.[10] As he explains, the recent protests are different than those of the Green Movement in 2009, which were more about demands for political reforms and liberalization—protests which were successful in bringing about the reform presidency of Hassan Rouhani who was recently re-elected. As Prashad notes, Rouhani has eased "social sanctions" in Iran, where women now "openly sit in public without the veil," and Rouhani's secretary of the National Security Council announced that "restrictions on imprisoned reformist leaders would be lifted."

Prashad explains that "the current wave of protests . . . is an upsurge against the privations in Iran—unemployment [which is nearly 13 percent overall and around 50 percent for the youth], deprivation and hopelessness." And, these privations are the direct result of both the oil war and Western sanctions against Iran which have never really eased up, the nuclear deal with Iran notwithstanding.

As Prashad notes, Western sanctions against Iran—ostensibly in response to Iran's nuclear program—"cost Iran more than $160 billion in oil revenues since 2012. The penalty was borne by ordinary Iranians, who saw their standard of living fall and their aspirations for the future narrow." And, while President Rouhani promised economic improvements with the nuclear deal, "since the nuclear deal, the handcuffs on Iran remain. The U.S.—under Trump—tightened non-nuclear sanctions [in mid-2017]. Trump's belligerence towards Iran has stayed the hand of many transnational firms that had earlier expressed interest in making investments in Iran. Rouhani's bet has not really paid off. The 2015 nuclear deal . . . did not fully provide the kind of relief needed for the Iranian population. Expectations were raised, but little has been delivered."

Indeed, when I was in Iran, a number of people complained to me that while the Iranians have kept up their side of the nuclear deal, going so far as to pour concrete into their nuclear enrichment facilities, they have never received the benefits of the deal.

And, as I write these words, Trump has threatened to re-impose the nuclear sanctions against Iran in place prior to the nuclear deal which Iran has unquestionably abided by. Such a move will only increase the suffering of the Iranian people, but that has never appeared to be of concern for the powers that be in the United States.

In addition to the economic war, the United States has also been involved in supporting terrorist groups against Iran. The most notable such groups as the Mujahadeen e-Khalq ("MEK" or "MKO"), a longtime nemesis of the Islamic Republic and a group which the US State Department listed as a terrorist group back in 1992. Indeed, it was Saddam Hussein's support for the MEK which was a basis for the United States claiming that he was a state sponsor of terrorism.[11]

The United States' connivance with the MEK has been well known for some time. As Iranian scholar Trita Parsi explains, the United States' support for the MEK has been "an open secret in Washington. In late May 2003, ABC News reported that the Pentagon was calling for the overthrow of the Iranian regime by "using all available points of pressure on the Iranian regime, including backing armed Iranian dissidents and employing the services of the Mujahadeen e-Khalq."[12]

The website *Global Research* cites Ray Takeyh, senior fellow for the Council on Foreign Relations—the most influential US foreign policy think tank—for the proposition that the MEK is a "cult-like organization" with "totalitarian tendencies," going so far as to hold "many members against their will with the threat of death if ever they are caught attempting to escape."[13]

As *Global Research* further relates, "to this day MEK terrorists have been carrying out attacks inside Iran killing political opponents, attacking civilian targets, as well as carrying out the U.S.-Israeli program of targeting and assassinating Iranian scientists." Indeed, when I was in Iran, I was told that the Iranian government estimates that the MEK has carried out terrorist attacks within Iran killing around seventeen thousand people—that is, the equivalent of nearly six 9/11's in a country a quarter the size of the United States.

MEK's terrorist actions have not been limited to Iranian targets, but have also been aimed at Americans:

> MEK has carried out decades of brutal terrorist attacks, assassinations, and espionage against the Iranian government and its people, as well as targeting Americans including the attempted kidnapping of U.S. Ambassador Douglas MacArthur II, the attempted assassination of USAF Brigadier General Harold Price, the successful assassination of Colonel Paul Shaffer and Lieutenant Colonel Jack Turner, and the successful ambush and killing of American Rockwell employees William Cottrell, Donald Smith, and Robert Krongard.[14]

The MEK is also accused by the US State Department of having participated "in the 1979 takeover of the U.S. Embassy in Tehran and later argued against the release of the hostages." Then, after leaving Iran and joining up with Saddam Hussein in his war against Iran, the MEK took "part in the bloody crackdown on Iraqi Shiites and Kurds who rose up against Saddam Hussein's regime at the end of the first Gulf War in 1991."[15]

Given all of this, it may seem surprising that the MEK was de-listed as a terrorist organization by the Obama Administration in 2012. Again, consider this when assessing Obama's sincerity in later agreeing to the nuclear deal with Iran. As Tony Cartalucci notes, de-listing a still-active terrorist group which targets Iran shortly before signing what appears to be a peace deal with Iran seems suspicious at best.[16]

Far from being treated as the brutal terrorist group it is, the MEK has now been given the stamp of approval by the United States. For example, John Bolton, former US Ambassador to the UN under George W. Bush and now President Trump's national security adviser, addressed the MEK conference in Paris, France, in July 2017 when I happened to be in Iran. At this conference, Bolton made it clear that he backed the MEK and that he said expressly that Trump must work toward regime change in Iran so that the Islamic Republic would not reach its fortieth birthday (in February 2019). Bolton has indeed been openly calling for war with Iran for some time, and he now holds a critical position in the Trump Administration from which he could start it.

And sadly, as the *American Conservative* magazine noted in 2015,[17] "Bolton is hardly the only former official, retired officer, or ex-politician to do this [Rudi Giuliani, Newt Gingrich, Democrat Howard Dean, former CIA directors Porter Goss and James Woolsley, and former Homeland Security Director Tom Ridge are others],[18] but for the last several years he has been a vocal cheerleader of the Mujahideen-e Khalq cult (and 'former' terrorist group) and its political organization. He has consistently misrepresented a totalitarian cult as a 'democratic' Iranian opposition group," though it "has absolutely no support in its own country in order to achieve regime change."

And, of course, Bolton and others were aided in this effort by then

Secretary of State Hillary Clinton who removed them "from the terrorist list in 2012 after a campaign that included both Democratic and Republican politicians, some of whom received sizable fees to speak to the exile's group annual gatherings."[19] The MEK even has an office in Washington, DC now.

This should not be too surprising given the United States' support for other terrorist groups which have done even greater harm around the world, including to US persons and interests. And again, the United States has been supporting these other terrorist groups largely to weaken Iran.

* * *

While those bent upon Iran's demise often accuse it of being a state sponsor of terrorism, and while recent US sanctions on Iran are premised upon this claim, there is certainly no evidence that Iran is supporting terrorism against the United States. As Lawrence Wilkerson, former CIA analyst and top National Security Council member under George W. Bush, recently explained in an op-ed in the *New York Times*:

> Today, the analysts claiming close ties between al-Qaeda and Iran come from the Foundation for Defense of Democracies, which vehemently opposes the Iran nuclear deal and unabashedly calls for regime change in Iran.
>
> It seems not to matter that 15 of the 19 hijackers on Sept. 11 were Saudis and none were Iranians. Or that, according to the United States intelligence community, of the groups listed as actively hostile to the United States, only one is loosely affiliated with Iran, and Hezbollah doesn't make the cut. More than ever the Foundation for Defense of Democracies seems like the Pentagon's Office of Special Plans that pushed falsehoods in support of waging war with Iraq.[20]

Indeed, the claim that Iran is linked to al-Qaeda is particularly galling given that Iran vigorously denounced the 9/11 attacks, is a sworn enemy of al-Qaeda, and indeed helped the United States with the war on terror after 9/11. But of course, nothing the United States has done in the Middle East makes any sense in the context of a war on terror or a rational response to 9/11.

Thus in 2003 the United States, claiming to be acting in response to the 9/11 attacks, finally deposed Saddam Hussein in the second US invasion of that country—though it is clear that Hussein had nothing to do with the 9/11 attacks, and the United States was quite aware of this fact.

One of the quite predictable consequences of the ousting of Saddam Hussein, who had imposed minority Sunni rule over the majority Shiite population, was to bring a Shiite government into power. This government, also not surprisingly, then found a friend in neighboring Shiite Iran. The United States then panicked at Iran's resulting ascendancy in the Middle East and aimed at doing something to undo this.

What the United States did next was best explained by Pulitzer-prize winning journalist Seymour Hersh in his March 5, 2007, article entitled "The Redirection: Is the Administration's new policy benefitting our enemies in the war on terrorism?"[21] This article turned out to be quite prescient and helpful in understanding the current conflict in the Middle East.

In this piece, Hersh explains how, in the mid-2000s, the United States was already shifting its policy away from its post-9/11 "war on terror" which purported to attack Sunni extremists (e.g., al-Qaeda) and instead toward attacking Shiite organizations and governments in the Middle East in order to weaken Iran, which it had just strengthened with its 2003 invasion of Iraq. And, the United States waged these anti-Shia attacks with the help of the very Sunni extremists we claimed to be at war with.

As Hersh writes in the aftermath of the fall of Saddam Hussein, "The U.S. has also taken part in clandestine operations aimed at Iran and its ally Syria. A by-product of these activities has been the bolstering of Sunni extremist groups that espouse a militant vision of Islam and are hostile to America and sympathetic to al-Qaeda."

Obama continued this policy of George W. Bush, thus aligning with jihadists in Libya to topple Muammar Gaddafi—one of the most aggressive enemies of al-Qaeda and with Sunni extremists in Syria in order to topple, or at least weaken, the Syrian government in Damascus and then pave the way for toppling Syria's ally, Iran.

Indeed, as journalist Ben Norton explains, it was just revealed by Obama's former ambassador to Syria, Robert S. Ford, that the United States spent $12 billion from 2014 to 2017 in regime-change efforts in Syria, contradicting claims by supporters of the Syrian opposition that Obama "did nothing" in Syria during this time.[22] And, this figure most likely does not include additional monies spent by the CIA on such efforts.

Ben Norton cites the *New York Times* for the proposition that "the CIA program in Syria was 'one of the most expensive efforts to arm and train rebels since the agency's program arming the mujahedeen in Afghanistan during the 1980's,' which gave birth to al-Qaeda and the Taliban." For his part, former ambassador Ford was one of the officials who also busted the "moderate Syrian rebel" myth, decrying the fact that the rebels the US was supporting in Syria were closely collaborating with, and indeed backed by, al-Qaeda and ISIS.[23]

As for Libya, the United States and other countries of the West served as the air force for the extremist groups trying to overthrow Gaddafi in 2011. And, they did so knowing that this could, and probably would, result in an extremist takeover of Libya. For example, in an email between then Secretary of State Hillary Clinton, one of the architects of the Libyan invasion, and close adviser Sydney Blumenthal, Blumenthal explains that "traditionally, the eastern part of Libya has been a stronghold for radical Islamist groups, including the al-Qaida linked Libyan Islamic Fighting Group. While Qaddafi's regime has been successful in suppressing the jihadist threat in Libya, the current situation [meaning the NATO intervention] opens the door for jihadist resurgence."[24]

I actually met Gaddafi's last foreign minister, Khaled Kaim, in Caracas, Venezuela, and he made a point to tell me that he personally warned US officials at the UN Security Council that they would open up a Pandora's box of extremism if they went ahead with their plans for intervention and regime change. He also asked for a one-hour delay of the commencement of the NATO bombing to allow for an inspection of Benghazi to confirm that there was no humanitarian crisis there as was being alleged to justify the intervention. Kaim was ignored on both counts by US officials, who were committed to war at any cost.

And, as predicted, if not intended, the jihadist resurgence took place, with violent extremists taking over Libya and then moving on to other countries like Mali, Tunisia, and Syria. In addition, a member of the Libyan Islamic Fighting Group, which NATO effectively part-nered with during the Libyan operation, ended up committing an act of terrorism in Great Britain with an improvised bombing of the Manchester Arena, killing twenty-two people including women and children.[25]

In January of 2018, US Secretary of State Rex Tillerson announced that we will be staying in northern Syria indefinitely, not to counter ISIS or al-Qaeda, but instead, to counter Iran. What is curious, again, is that while it is true that Iran has been intervening in Syria, it has done so legally, upon the invitation of the sovereign Syrian govern-ment, which is not true of the United States' unilateral intervention. Moreover, Iran has been fighting the same forces that the United States has claimed it is fighting—namely, ISIS and al-Qaeda. As one commentator reasonably queried:

> As with anything the Trump administration mentions about the Mid-
> dle East, there is always the bogeyman of Iran. And as usual, Iran is

described in general pejoratives—the lead adjective on the subject in
[Secretary of State] Tillerson's speech [about the U.S.'s decision to
stay in Syria] was "malignant"—without addressing exactly how
Iran's position in, and relationship with, Syria threatens any U.S.
interests. Nor was there any recognition of the inconsistency of justifying a U.S. military intervention that was supposed to be about
opposing IS by talking about malignancy on the part of a regional
power [Iran] that itself has been opposing IS, in Iraq as well as
Syria.[26]

In terms of Iran's anti-terrorist operations in Iraq, even some mainstream news sources have had to admit that, with the permission of the
Iraqi government, Iran has been supporting thousands of Shia militias
in Iraq who are "essential to the fight" against ISIS and al-Qaeda
there.[27]

Meanwhile, it is generally accepted that ISIS directly grew out of
the US invasion of Iraq in 2003 and the mistreatment of Iraqi detainees by the US following the intervention. Thus, as NPR recently noted,
ISIS was originally led and manned by former Iraqi detainees who
were radicalized by their abuse at the hands of the US military. In the
words of NPR's Lulu Garcia-Navarro, "ISIS actually evolved out of a
U.S. detention center," and is thus "a monster of our own making."[28]

What's more, ISIS continues to be a US monster as the United
States has made common cause with ISIS and al-Qaeda in its low-
intensity war against Iran.

Quite revealing is a document put out by the US Defense Intelligence Agency (DIA), an external intelligence service of the United
States federal government specializing in defense and military intelligence. In this document, dated August 2012, and later declassified and
provided to Judicial Watch pursuant to a FOIA request, the DIA makes
it clear that Russia, China, and Iran are supporting the Syrian government, while "the West [namely, the United States and Israel], Gulf
countries, and Turkey support the opposition."[29] The document goes

on to explain that al-Qaeda—Iraq (AQI) "supported the Syrian opposition from the beginning," corroborating President Assad's claims that terrorists were involved with the opposition uprising from the very outset.

The DIA further explains that AQI is opposed to the Syrian government and wages war upon it because it regards "Syria as an infidel regime for its support of the infidel Party Hezbollah, and other [Shiite] regimes he considers dissenters like Iran and Iraq."

Incredibly, the DIA goes on to state, indeed to admit, that "if the situation unravels there is the possibility of establishing a declared or undeclared Salafist principality in eastern Syria (Hasaka and Der Zor), and this is exactly what the supporting powers to the opposition want, in order to isolate the Syrian regime, which is considered the strategic depth of Shia expansion (Iraq and Iran)."

Of course, when the DIA states that the "supporting powers to the opposition" want the establishment of a Salafist principality (or, Caliphate) to counter Iran and Iraq, it means that the United States and Israel, among others, desire this. In other words, while we have been led to believe the United States is sending our soldiers to fight and die overseas to take on the terrorists, the United States is actually supporting the terrorists. And, equally horrifying, the DIA makes it clear that the United States welcomes the unraveling of the situation to bring about the Salafist principality in Syria; in other words, chaos is the desired means to the United States' desired end, which appears to be . . . more chaos!

Indeed, "former director of the Defense Intelligence Agency Michael Flynn confirms . . . that not only had he studied the DIA memo predicting the West's backing of an Islamic State in Syria when it came across his desk in 2012, but even asserts that the White House's sponsoring of radical jihadists (that would emerge as ISIL and Nusra) against the Syrian regime was 'a willful decision.'"[30]

In 2015, President Obama himself confirmed the statements in the DIA document as well as Flynn's assessment of it, making clear his intention to merely "contain" ISIS, rather than to destroy it as he originally promised, given that, in his assessment, outright destroying ISIS at that time would be counterproductive to the United States' interest of unseating Syrian President Assad and confronting Iran—again, as with the Iran-Iraq war, the goal has been to keep the conflict at a slow burn, without putting out the fire altogether, so as to weaken and bleed all parties.[31]

Henry Kissinger—who should be in jail given his overseeing many a war crime from Vietnam, Laos, and Cambodia to Chile, but who is now treated as an elder statesman—recently warned Trump that he should not destroy ISIS altogether lest Iran be strengthened in the process.[32] Speaking for many in the US foreign policy establishment, Kissinger opined that, while countries such as Iran believe we should finish off ISIS and would gladly help us do it, an ascendant Iran is even more dangerous and permitting ISIS to exist may help prevent this. Sounding like the madman he is, Kissinger said that "the enemy of your enemy may also be your enemy."[33]

This policy of "containment," rather than the outright destruction, of ISIS has borne the desired fruit, with Iran now suffering "the kind of terrorist attacks that have hit Arab and Western capitals."[34] This was seen most dramatically with the ISIS attack in June of 2017 upon the Iranian parliament and mausoleum of the Ayatollah Khomeini. This took place just before my visit to Iran and was very much a topic of conversation there, with many opining that this attack was ultimately the handiwork of the United States.

Of course, there are terrible potential consequences for this dance with the devil, especially if this devil cannot be contained. Indeed, the DIA predicted in its August 2012 document one such dire consequence which did come to pass shortly thereafter. As the DIA explained, AQI's setting up a Salafist state in Syria with US support "creates the ideal atmosphere for AQI to return to its old pockets in Mosul and Ramadi, and will provide a renewed momentum under the presumption of unifying the Jihad among Sunni Iraq and Syria, and the rest of the Sunnis in the Arab world against what it considers one enemy, the Dissenters [most notably Iran and the government of Iraq]. ISI could also declare an Islamic state through its union with other terrorist organizations in Iraq and Syria, which will create grave danger in regards to unifying Iraq and the protection of its territory."

As we all know, the extremists, in the form of the Islamic State in Iraq and Syria (ISIS), did just what the DIA predicted, returning to Mosul, Iraq, and declaring a Caliphate in Syria and Iraq in June of 2014. They would go on to wreak havoc in Mosul and terrorize the population. With the genie that the United States helped conjure now out of the bottle, US coalition forces, after waiting over a year and a half for sufficient damage to be done, commenced an aggressive bombing campaign in February of 2017 to oust ISIS from Mosul.

There are estimates of at least forty thousand civilians killed in what has come to be known as the Battle of Mosul.[35] This battle was marked by major war crimes committed on all sides of the conflict as Amnesty International (AI) reported in its 2017 report, "At Any Cost: The Civilian Catastrophe in West Mosul, Iraq."[36]

For its part, according to AI, ISIS "summarily killed hundreds, if not thousands, of men, women and children as they attempted to flee and hanged their bodies in public areas." ISIS also moved thousands of civilians into the zone of combat, effectively using them as human shields. In addition, ISIS denied the civilian population food, water, and access to medical care. By the end of the nearly six-month battle, civilians were feeding off of underground spelt and grass to survive. Meanwhile, ISIS nearly wiped out Iraq's Counter-Terrorism Service, killing between four to six thousand of their eight thousand total troops.

Not to be outdone, the Coalition forces, led by the United States, indiscriminately bombed huge swaths of Mosul, killing at least 5,800 civilians in the process. According to Amnesty International, the indiscriminate and disproportionate nature of this bombing most certainly constituted a war crime.

One such example of US war crimes was the March 17, 2017, bombing of West Mosul which killed at least 137, and possibly as many as 500, civilians. The *Washington Post* would later describe this as one of the worst US-led civilian bombings in the past twenty-five years. As the *Post* explained, this one bombing "could possibly rank [as] one of the most devastating attacks on civilians by American forces in more than two decades."[37]

By design, the United States, through its policy of playing one Middle East country against another and of at various times creating, supporting, or just tolerating various terrorist groups, has unleashed indescribable chaos upon the region. This has not only caused untold loss of life and suffering to the people of the region, but has also led to the eradication of their history and culture.

Here is but a partial list of the destruction that ISIS, the sometimes ally of the United States in its quest to undermine Iran, has wrought in just Iraq and Syria alone: in Mosul, Iraq, ISIS blew up the Great Mosque of al-Nuri and its leaning minaret, trashed the Mosul museum as well as other museums and libraries, and dynamited Christian churches and mosques; in nearby Nineva, an ancient Assyrian city on the outskirts of Mosul, it destroyed many of the ancient ruins and antiquities; in other parts of Iraq, ISIS has destroyed the fourth century Catholic Mar Behnam Monastery, the Mosque of the Prophet Yunus, and the Imam Dur Mausoleum; in Palmyra, Syria, ISIS destroyed ancient Roman ruins, such as the Temple of Baalshamin and the Temple of Baal; and elsewhere in Syria ISIS has destroyed such treasures as the Christian Mar Elian Monastery.[38]

Meanwhile, the United States itself has also done a great job of destroying vast swaths of countries like Afghanistan, Iraq, Libya, and Syria too, and ancient artifacts therein. For example, the US invasions of Iraq have opened that country's, and in truth the world's, antiquities for mass looting, and the US forces have done nothing to stop this. As Noam Chomsky points out, after the US invasion of Iraq in 2003,

The Pentagon officials in charge did make sure that other sites were protected, however: the oil and security ministries. Elsewhere, looting and destruction, including of irreplaceable treasures of civilization, proceeded unconstrained. Two years after the invasion, the president of the American Academic Research Institute in Iraq, Macguire Gibson, sadly confirmed that 'Iraq is losing its culture and its wealth.' By then, more than half of the nation's archeological sites, including most major Sumerian ones, had been destroyed. 'The Americans are not doing anything,' Gibson added. . . . The losses at these sites dwarfed even the massive looting of the National Museum shortly after the US troops arrived, in which at least 15,000 to 20,000 looted pieces disappeared, probably forever.[39]

Israel too is engaged in its own campaign of mass destruction, particularly of what is left of the Palestinian people. Thus, with the complicity of the United States, Israel is literally starving out the Palestinians, particularly those who occupy the Gaza Strip, in what is clearly an act of slow-moving genocide. Indeed, betraying Israel's genocidal intent, Israel's Defense Minister, Avigdor Lieberman, recently stated that there are "no innocent people in Gaza"; this intent is being manifest in the collective punishment of all of Gaza.

As Amnesty International explains in its most recent annual report,

Gaza [has] remained under an Israeli air, sea and land blockade, in force since June 2007. The continuing restrictions on imports of construction materials under the blockade, and funding shortages, contributed to severe delays in reconstruction of homes and other infrastructure damaged or destroyed in recent armed conflicts. Continuing restrictions on exports crippled the economy and exacerbated widespread impoverishment among Gaza's 1.9 million inhabitants. The Egyptian authorities' almost total closure of the Rafah border crossing with Gaza completed its isolation and compounded the impact of the Israeli blockade.

According to the United Nations which puts it quite bluntly, Gaza will be "unlivable" by 2020—that is, in just a couple short years. As the UN explains, "Gaza has continued on its trajectory of 'de-development,' in many cases even faster than we had originally projected." One of the biggest issues confronting Gaza, the UN explains, is the near total lack of electricity for its residents, which makes keeping food and many life-saving medicines impossible.

The truth is that, for many, Gaza is already unlivable. In a recent interview in the Israeli paper *Haaretz* entitled "Gaza Kids Live in Hell: A Psychologist Tells of Rampant Sexual Abuse, Drugs and Despair," trauma treatment expert Mohammed Mansour relates that the situation in Gaza has taken a drastic turn for the worse even in recent months. Dr. Mansour explains, in his most recent visit,

> I encountered a large number of cases of sexual abuse among the children. That's a phenomenon that has always existed, but in this visit, and also in the previous visit, in August, it suddenly reached far larger dimensions. It's become positively huge. More than one-third of the children I saw in the Jabalya [refugee] camp reported being sexually abused. Children from ages 5 to 13.

Dr. Manour makes it abundantly clear that it is the Israeli blockade and the resulting "de-development" of Gaza that is leading to this dire situation:

> Most people don't work, and those who do, earn pennies—the average salary is 1,000 shekels a month [$285]. Mentally and physically, parents are simply not capable of supporting their children. They are immersed in their own depression, their own trauma. . ..
>
> I've seen the starvation. I visit meager, empty homes. The refrigerator is off even during the hours when they have electric power, because there's nothing in it. The children tell me that they eat once a day; some eat once every two days.

As Dr. Manour concluded, "The trauma does not end and will not end. Adults and children live in terrible pain, they're only looking for how to escape it. We also see growing numbers of addicts."[40]

As the UN Development Program (UNDP) determined in a series of *Arab Development Reports*, the Israeli occupation of Palestine has, among other things such as the US invasion of Iraq, "'adversely influenced' human development."[41]

Meanwhile, President Trump has suspended $65 million of aid to the United Nations Relief and Works Agency for Palestine Refugees in the Near East (UNRWA), and is backing out of giving another $45 million of aid for food to the Palestinians. Even hard-liners in Israel have complained that this amounts to a death sentence for thousands of Palestinians.

Not content to merely wipe out the Palestinian people, Israel is also bent on destroying their cultural heritage, even going so far as to claim that the Palestinians have no heritage or history of their own to begin with. Indeed, a book last year which quickly shot to number one in Amazon's "Middle East History" category, before being pulled from the website, was *A History of the Palestinian People: From Ancient Times to the Modern Era* by Israeli author Assaf Voll.[42] This book, which purported to be "the comprehensive and extensive review of some 3,000 years of Palestinian history" consisted of 120 blank pages—a cruel joke attempting to show that the Palestinians have no history. Apparently, for many, it is not enough that Israel is destroying the Palestinian people; it must also destroy any memory of them, as well.

This is reminiscent of the scene in Gabriel Garcia Marquez's *One Hundred Years of Solitude* when, after a banana strike was crushed by the Colombian military and the strikers killed, the banana company (in real life, the United Fruit Company in the town of Ciénaga, Colombia in 1928) had all of the strikers' bodies loaded onto railcars and taken away. Eventually, the strikers, the strike, and even the banana company itself, which ended up abandoning the area, were forgotten by the people of the town.

I fear that a time may come soon when the people, culture, traditions, religion, and ancient architecture of the Islamic world are ground into oblivion and then forgotten.

Another sign that this may be the endgame as far as the United States in particular is concerned is the United States' long-time war with UNESCO—the UN agency tasked with preserving world cultural sites—and President Trump's recent announcement that the United States was backing out of UNESCO entirely and would not pay the $550 million it already owes to that agency.[43]

And, not surprisingly, the United States made this decision precisely because UNESCO was doing its job in trying to preserve Palestinian culture from destruction. As the *New York Times* explains, the United States' decision was in response to the fact that "in July, UNESCO declared the ancient and hotly contested core of Hebron, in the Israeli-occupied West Bank, as a Palestinian World Heritage site in danger, a decision sharply criticized by Israel and its allies. And in 2015, UNESCO adopted a resolution that criticized Israel for mishandling heritage sites in Jerusalem and condemned 'Israeli aggressions and illegal measures against freedom of worship.'" The destruction of the Palestinian people and culture must go on, as far as the United States is concerned.

In the foregoing ways, ISIS, the United States, and Israel seem to have similar intentions, at least in the short run, and that is to destroy the Middle East as we know it. Maybe the plan is to make it into a giant oil refinery, with some poppy fields on the side, or to turn it into an appendage of Europe and/or Israel. Maybe the idea is to destroy all of the Middle East's capacity for oil production so that the world will have to depend upon US fossil fuel production, now the greatest in the world. Or, maybe the idea is to turn it into a giant parking lot as some like Ronald Reagan had advocated for Vietnam, famously saying that "we could pave the whole country and put parking strips on it, and still be home by Christmas." In any case, the goal appears to be to wipe out what and who is there now.

In truth, it is Iran which is one of the few countries standing in the way of this nihilistic project by promoting a humane version of Islam, fighting the very terrorists the United States merely claims to be fighting, and trying to bring stability to neighboring countries such as Iraq.

Indeed, as Middle East expert Vali Nasr related recently in *Foreign Affairs*, "Without Iran's military reach and the strength of its network of allies and clients in Iraq and Syria, ISIS would have quickly swept through Damascus, Baghdad, and Erbil (the capital of Iraqi's Kurdistan), before reaching Iran's own borders." [44] In other words, what the United States and Israel usually term Iran's sponsorship of terrorism is in fact a fight against terrorism, and an effective one at that. However, given the United States' and Israel's general confusion between wars on terror and wars for terror, this mistake is not surprising.

Meanwhile, during the times that the United States is in the mood to confront ISIS, it will sometimes appear to be working in concert with Iran in doing so. As Patrick Cockburn has explained, for example:

> In Iraq the US and Iranians are still publicly denouncing each other, but when Iranian-controlled Shia militias attacked north Baghdad in September [of 2014] to end the ISIS siege of the Shia Turkoman town of Amerli, their advance was made possible by US air strikes on ISIS positions. When the discredited Iraqi prime minister Nouri al-Maliki was replaced by Haider al-Abadi during the same period, the change was backed by both Washington and Tehran. [45]

In short, if the United States really wants to fight terrorism and to bring stability to the Middle East, it would appear that Iran would be a worthy partner with which to do this.

This, of course, begs the question of why Iran is such a big bugaboo for the United States and why it is seemingly bent on finding pretexts to justify attacking it. To answer this question, I would submit, we must go back about seventy-five years to the very beginning of the United States' relationship with Iran and to the fount of the discord between these two countries.

3

THE UNITED STATES AND UNITED KINGDOM DESTROY IRANIAN DEMOCRACY

MY TWO SONS HAVE GONE TO public school in Pittsburgh throughout grade school and secondary education. While they were in grade school, the superintendent of Pittsburgh Public Schools was Mark Roosevelt, a quite innovative and erudite individual who moved here from Boston. Roosevelt, who served as superintendent between 2005 and 2010, had the unenviable and unpopular job of overseeing the closing and consolidation of numerous schools in order to rescue the cash-strapped school district. While it was often pointed out with great pride that Mark is the great-grandchild of President Teddy Roosevelt, it was rare that Mark's father was ever mentioned. It was his father, however, who played a key and fateful role in the history of Iran and in the trajectory of US-Iranian relations for many years to come, Mark's father being the legendary Kermit Roosevelt—the CIA bureau chief in Tehran who led the coup against Iranian Prime Minister Mohammad Mossadegh in 1953.

The CIA-led coup against Mossadegh has been written about extensively, including by Kermit Roosevelt himself in his tell-all and self-serving book, *Countercoup: The Struggle for the Control of Iran* (1981). However, it was not until 2017 that the Bureau of Public Affairs of the US State Department released a huge trove of documents revealing the CIA's role in the coup.[1] As one author, describing a more limited release of CIA documents in 2013, explains, "The documents' existence and contents contrast sharply with a report in the *New York Times* in 1997 that quoted CIA officials stating falsely that most of the documents relating to Iran in 1953 were either lost or destroyed in the early 1960's, allegedly because the record-holders' safes were too full."[2]

The documents released in 2017, containing recently-declassified information (though much is still classified), are quite instructive, for they show how our government officials can hold completely contradictory ideas in their minds at the same time (for example, that the Soviet Union was a threat to US interests in Iran when on the very next page they conclude that it really was not), and then formulate policies and actions based upon these ideas. The resulting policies and actions, when viewed dispassionately, seem to make no sense at all, and do not even seem reasonably aimed at accomplishing the stated goals (e.g., democracy and freedom). But sadly, and incredibly, the self-contradictory nature of such policies is never pointed out, either by government officials, by the press, or by educators, and so our nation continues to act out in ways that can only be described as irrational and insane, and which result in utter disaster for everyone involved.

For over the past century, Iran's greatest resource, and at the same time its greatest curse, has been its oil. In 1901, the corrupt Iranian monarch, Muzaffar al-Din Shah, sold the entirety of Iran's oil and natural gas rights for a mere twenty-thousand pounds to William Knox D'Arcy, a financier based in London.[3] In 1908, D'Arcy's concession was reconfigured as the Anglo Persian Oil Company (APOC), 51 percent of which was later bought by the British government.

Meanwhile, in 1906, inspired by the Russian Revolution of 1905, the people of Iran (then called Persia) rose up to challenge the power of the Shah, and their uprising was crushed by both Great Britain and czarist Russia, the czar of Russia having violently crushed his own people's attempted revolution as well.

The one concrete thing to come out of this revolt was an elected parliament known as the Majlis, which has existed since then and to the present time, subject to being suspended at times, in various forms and with various degrees of authority.

Then, in 1907, Russia and the United Kingdom drew up the Anglo-Russian Convention of 1907, which divided Iran into two parts; Russia received the north and Britain the South, and the Shah was left with a small piece in the middle. This partitioning was done without Iran even participating in the discussions.

After the 1917 Russian Revolution, the Soviet Union renounced most of its rights in Iran and canceled the country's debts owed to the czar.

Meanwhile, pursuant to the "harsh Anglo-Persian Agreement of 1919" which gave the British "control over Iran's army, treasury, transport system, and communications network,"[4] the APOC continued to extract Iran's oil and to refine it in the world's largest oil refinery on the island of Abadan at the north end of the Persian Gulf, and to ship it out of the country for sale. As one commentator notes, "Not only was the oil a source of fabulous wealth for the British, it also gave them the edge in the world as both an industrial and naval power."[5]

However, Iran's oil wealth was not benefitting its people, who still lived in abject poverty. This was due to the fact that "Tehran was only earning between ten and twelve percent in royalties on APOC's net proceeds, which meant that the British government was making far more revenue from Iranian oil than the Iranian government." To make matters worse, most of APOC's Iranian workers were poorly paid and housed in bad conditions. As Stephen Dorril describes, the company effectively operated as though "it was still the nineteenth century, regarding Iranians as merely wogs."[6] Kermit Roosevelt would acknowledge later, just after the 1953 coup, that 90 percent of the Iranian population was illiterate even at that time.[7]

Indeed, as D. F. Fleming explains in his lost classic *The Cold War and Its Origins*, the people of Iran were kept "in a state of squalor unequaled in the world."[8] Fleming relates that "in some villages 90 percent of the people had malaria, and infant mortality exceeded 50 percent." Iran, according to Fleming, was truly "'a nation in rags.' Abject misery was graven on most faces. Even in Teheran anyone standing on the street would be approached by a beggar every five minutes."

In 1921, the British engineered a coup against the Shah in power at that time, and by 1926, a new Shah, Reza Shah, had consolidated his position. It was Reza Shah who changed the name of Persia to Iran (literally, "land of the Arians") in the 1930s. While the British still controlled Iran's oil industry, they left it to Reza Shah to run the government and military.

While Reza Shah tried to modernize the country, he used brutal methods against the population and was a Nazi sympathizer.[9] Reza Shah soon decided to align Iran with Nazi Germany and invited hundreds of Germans into Iran to help with the construction of factories, roads, bridges, and other buildings. As Ryszard Kapuscinsi explains in his *Shah of Shahs*, "The Shah admired Hitler and surrounded himself with Hitler's people. There were Germans all over Iran, in the palace, the ministries, the army. The Abwehr [Germany military intelligence] became a force to reckon with in Teheran, and the Shah looked on approvingly."

When I was in Iran, it was explained to me that the Nazis actually helped build a prison in the early 1930s which became a torture center for the Iranian security apparatus (known as the SAVAK) set up by the CIA in 1957. Upon my own request, I visited this prison, now the Ebrat Museum, while in Tehran. We were led on a tour of the center (preserved as it had been while being run by the SAVAK) by a man who had himself been imprisoned there and tortured by the SAVAK.

One of the cells contains a life-sized mannequin made to resemble current Supreme Leader of Iran, Ayatollah Ali Khamenei, who spent eight months in that very prison cell and who suffered greatly at the hands of the SAVAK. In addition, many of the rooms are still adorned just as they would have been before 1979, with the framed photos of the last Shah of Iran, along with his beautiful wife and his young son. Many of the halls are lined with row after row of photos of the thousands of other inmates of this prison, many of whom never made it out of there in one piece, if at all.

Of course, there were many Iranians at the time who abhorred the Nazis and their war against Jews and ethnic minorities. One such Iranian was Abdol-Hossein Sardari, who was the head of Iran's diplomatic mission in Paris, France, at the time of the Nazi invasion. Sardari, today known as the "Iranian Schindler," would use his position there, and the Iranian government's good graces with Germany at the time, to save over two thousand Iranian Jews [over twice the number of Jews saved by Schindler himself] who were trapped in occupied France.[10] He provided these individuals "with the passports and travel documents they needed for safe-passage through Nazi-occupied Europe," and back to Iran which, despite the government's relationship with Germany, was still a safe place for Jews to reside. In his work, and even in communications to the Nazis, Sardari appealed to Iranian history, and in particular to the reign of "the Persian Emperor Cyrus [who] had freed Jewish exiles in Babylon in 538 BC" and allowed them to return to their homes.

In 1941, the British and the Soviets invaded Iran to oust the Germans, and Iran then signed a treaty with the Allies. At that time, the Shah was also forced to abdicate his throne, and his son, Mohammed Reza Pahlavi, was sworn in as the new Shah of Iran. Mohammed Reza Pahlavi would ultimately be the last Shah of Iran. Meanwhile, Abdol-Hossein Sardari, who was then recalled by the Iranian government from his post as a diplomat in occupied France, nonetheless stayed in Paris, at great peril to himself, to continue his humanitarian work of saving Iranian Jews and others.[11]

It was against this backdrop that, in the early 1950s, the people of Iran united around a talented, nationalist politician to try to gain true independence—independence which necessarily included more Iranian control over its precious oil resources. The politician's name was Mohammed Mossadegh.

Mossadegh, upon being elected to the Majlis' oil committee, and suspecting that the British were shortchanging the Iranians on the oil royalties owed them, initially made the quite reasonable request for the British to open Anglo Persian's financial books. The British refused this request as well as Mossadegh's request to train Iranians in technical jobs of the oil industry. When Mossadegh was elected head of the Majlis' oil committee, he then demanded that Iran receive half the profits of the Anglo Persian Oil Company. Again, Britain refused.

It was only after the British refusals of these reasonable requests that the Majlis, under the leadership of Mossadegh who was elected prime minister by overwhelming vote of the Majlis on April 28, 1951, finally decided to nationalize Iran's oil industry on May 1, 1951. As one commentator points out, it was at this very time that Britain was beginning to nationalize its own coal, electric rail, and steel industries, under the leadership of the Labor Party which had been the governing party since the end of WWII.[12] But what was good for the goose was not good for the gander, and so, in retaliation for Iran's nationalization, the British stopped exporting refined oil from the Abbadan refinery, and Iran, without tankers or oil technicians of its own, could neither run the refinery nor export any oil.

Once Winston Churchill returned as UK prime minister in October of 1951, Britain took even more aggressive action against Mossadegh, buying off Iranian media and undermining the country's economy.[13]

At this point, the British Empire was in its death throes, and Britain was attempting to cling to at least some of its empire with all of its might. In addition to countries like Iran, Britain in the early 1950s was also attempting to subjugate countries like Kenya, where Britain would attempt to wipe out the rebellious Kikuyu ethnic group. As has recently been exposed, the United Kingdom, under Churchill's leadership, imprisoned 1.5 million Kikuyu in "a network of detention camps," much like Stalin's gulags, where they "suffered forced labour, disease, starvation, torture, rape and murder."[14] Possibly hundreds of thousands of Kikuyu died in what some, including historian Caroline Elkins, have termed Britain's genocidal campaign against them.[15] Ironically, while Churchill decried Stalin's gulags, and warned of the USSR's "Iron Curtain" descending upon Eastern Europe, he had no qualms about his own gulags in Africa.

Still, Britain's empire was on the wane, while the United States' was on the rise. And so Britain, whose embassy had been shut down by Mossadegh after he learned of Britain's coup plans, turned to its faithful ally for help. Churchill was initially rebuffed by President Harry S. Truman, who simply had no interest in a project aimed at maximizing the United Kingdom's oil profits, and who himself was busy in a campaign of mass slaughter of his own in Korea. So, Churchill then turned to the newly-elected President Dwight D. Eisenhower for assistance.

Having learned from Truman's rebuke, PM Churchill, along with the newly-formed CIA under Allen Dulles who happened to be an associate of the firm providing legal counsel for APOC,[16] came up with a more tried and true pitch for getting rid of Mossadegh—rescuing Iran and the Middle East from the specter of Communism.[17] This sales point worked like a charm on Eisenhower, who readily green-lighted a US-instigated coup against Mossadegh. The coup plot was dubbed "Operation Ajax."

The coup plot was carried out by the CIA, headed by Allen Dulles, in close coordination with the US State Department, then headed by Allen's brother John, and the White House. It was collectively decided by these groups that they would reinstall the Shah, who Mossadegh had sidelined in the interest of trying to democratize Iran, and replace Mossadegh with General Fazlollah Zahedi in the prime minister position.

General Zahedi was known as a strongman, having been dismissed by Mossadegh from his position as minister of the interior after he "ordered the massacre" of protestors.[18] Zahedi also had a dark past, having been exiled by the British during WWII as a war profiteer and as a close friend of Nazi agents. While Steven Kinzer quotes British intelligence official "Monty" Woodhouse for the proposition that Zahedi "was an ironic choice, for during World War II he had been regarded as a German agent,"[19] this was not ironic at all.

Indeed, as evidenced in a CIA memo contained in the 2017 released documents, Zahedi's having been a Nazi collaborator was seen as an asset to the Americans. As the memo, detailing US assets in Iran, explains, "Associated with the Nazi efforts in Iran during World War II, he has long been firmly anti-Soviet. A pro-Western orientation is reflected in the education of his son in the U.S. and the activity of his son in the Point IV [Truman's Cold War technical assistance plan to developing countries] in Iran. . . ." The memo goes on to say that the CIA's contacts in Iran believed Zahedi "to be the only military man on the scene who would stage a coup and follow it through with forcefulness."[20]

This view, that being Nazi and resolutely anti-Soviet/anti-Communist go hand-in-hand, thus making a Nazi a potentially good partner for the United States, was then, and in some instances, continues to be, the prevailing view of US foreign policy leaders, particularly in the CIA. I remind readers here of Operation Paperclip, a plan instituted just after WWII pursuant to which

more than 1,600 Germans were secretly recruited to develop armaments "at a feverish and paranoid pace that came to define the Cold War."

Although some of these men had been Nazi Party members, SS officers and war criminals, they were valued as vital to American national security. Thus it was O.K., American government officials reasoned, to ignore these scientists' roles in developing biological and chemical weapons, in designing the V-2 rockets that shattered London and Antwerp and in the countless deaths of concentration camp inmates who fell victim to medical experiments at Dachau and Ravensbrück.[21]

In Japan, meanwhile, the United States quickly moved to restore fascist-era leaders to power to ensure that Japan would not turn to socialism, and so that it would be a reliable ally in suppressing anti-colonial movements in Korea, Vietnam, and Indonesia. The chief leader the United States selected to secure its interests in Japan and the Pacific was Nobusuke Kishi, also known as the "Shōwa (Emperor) era monster/devil"—the war criminal, famous for his brutality, who oversaw the use of coerced Korean and Chinese labor in Japan's Manchurian munitions factories.[22] The United States exonerated Kishi for his WWII-era war crimes, and he went on to serve two terms as Japan's prime minister in the 1950s, becoming widely known as "America's favorite war criminal."[23]

In addition, the United States and Britain got busy right after WWII in helping to install and prop up fascist regimes in countries like Greece as a bulwark against Communism.

And, of course, the stated goal of the United States intervention in Iran in 1953 was the prevention of a Communist takeover of Iran, either externally by the Soviet Union and/or internally by Iran's Communist Party (then and now known as the Tudeh Party). However, while the internal US documents show a concern about such a takeover, they also reveal the conclusion of key US policymakers that such a takeover was not a real threat or possibility at that time, and that the USSR would not act to try to counter the United States' coup attempt or to reverse it once the coup succeeded.

Thus, in the same CIA memo describing Zahedi's asset as a Nazi, the following assumptions about the coup plan are listed:

I. *Basic Assumptions*
    . . . 1. Mossadegh must go.

2. Appropriate U.S. covert assets will be directed toward his overthrow and U.S policy action and financial aid will support his successor. . . .

5. At this time Soviet reaction to a forced change in government would be limited in nature. . . .

7. Zahedi can last only if he manages the immediate removal of all dissident leaders. . . .

10. Zahedi's cabinet must include the strongest possible individuals, including a U.S. approved choice of his successor.[24]

In other words, as point five makes clear, the coup planners were quite aware that they could, and would, have their way with Iran without any significant interference from the Soviets.

In a Draft National Intelligence Estimate of the CIA, dated August 12, 1953, the CIA is even more pointed in its conclusions, stating that the Tudeh Party does not have the current capability to seize power nor the willingness to turn against Mossadegh, and therefore poses no threat.[25] The CIA also concludes that, despite the public pronouncements of the CIA's paid journalists that Mossadegh was some type of Communist stooge, "it is extremely unlikely that an ardent nationalist of Mossadegh's stripe would grant the USSR oil concessions, permit Soviet technicians to move into Abadan, or otherwise open the way for large-scale Soviet penetration of Iran. Moreover, it is almost equally unlikely that Mossadegh will sever all ties with the US."[26]

In short, Mossadegh's being in power was not a threat to the US interest of preventing Soviet expansion. The CIA acknowledges the Soviets' "paucity of military preparations and the probable unwillingness of the USSR to intervene militarily on its [Tudeh's] behalf."[27] And finally, the CIA, in another memo on April 17, acknowledges "Moscow's recent overtures of conciliation toward the West."[28] In the end, the CIA's assessment was correct, with the Soviet Union not making any moves in the eleventh hour of the coup to save the Mossadegh government.[29]

Thus, the CIA was quite aware that there was no internal or external Communist threat to Iran. Indeed, the CIA recognized that, to the extent Mossadegh was dealing with Russia at all, he was being forced to by the very circumstances in which the United States and Britain were putting him. Thus, in an August 6, 1953, internal embassy memo, Iranian Minister of National Economy A.A. Akhavi is quoted as saying that "there is no desire to have any relations with the neighbor to the north, including commercial relations, but that Iran was being forced to deal with Russia by reason of the fact that the United States and most of the free world would not buy its products."[30]

Another US Embassy memo, dated May 20, 1953, quotes Akhavi as stating that "if Iran is helped to become strong through the development of her resources, she will stand like a bastion of the free world in the Middle East because she is not involved in the Israel-Arab fight and is not conjoined with any neighboring country or its problems."[31] Of course, Iran today is decidedly involved "in the Israel-Arab fight," and is conjoined with neighboring states, most notably Lebanon. Quite possibly, if the United States had left well enough alone, Iran's role in the Middle East would be very different today.

In any case, Akhavi's claims were backed up at the time by British Ambassador Sir Roger Makins, who, in an August 17, 1953, telegram to Washington, says, "Whatever his faults Mussaddiq had no love for the Russians and timely aid might enable him to keep Communism in check."[32] It is important to note at this juncture that Sir Roger was pointing to an alternative here for both Britain and the United States—instead of going to the trouble of orchestrating a coup in a foreign land, they could have just helped Mossadegh and Iran move forward in the direction of Western, capitalist development. To put it in simplistic terms, they could have been nice, and probably obtained better results in the end.

Indeed, there are some moments in which doing something positive and helpful for Iran and the people of the Middle East was considered, if ever so briefly, as a path forward.

For example, in the March 4, 1953, meeting of the National Security Council, it is noted that "The President said in any case it was a matter of great distress to him that we seemed unable to get some of the people in these downtrodden countries to like us instead of hating us."[33]

In light of this statement, the following exchange took place:

> Mr. [Charles Douglas] Jackson [special assistant to Eisenhower and expert in psychological warfare] then said that he had another point which he felt would contribute to an improvement of our position in the Middle East and about which he felt it was possible to do something. This was American action to remove the festering sore in the Middle East represented by the 800,000 Arab displaced persons in Israel. . . . Mr. Jackson replied that it would certainly be possible to resettle 200,000 of these refugees, and that all 800,000 could at least be fed. The President added that it was not enough to feed them, but that he would be awfully glad if we could get some of the Arab countries to take these people if we would pay a subsidy of each head.[34]

In other words, the United States could improve its position in the Middle East by helping improve the lot of the Palestinian people who had been displaced in the 1948 creation of Israel. As Jackson mentioned, this was a "festering sore in the Middle East" even back then, and this sore continues to fester now. At this critical juncture, as the United States was just getting deeply involved in the Middle East for the first time, it could have decided to help and create in order to advance interests. Instead, it decided to destroy, and it would go on destroying despite other, more peaceful means being available. The result would be tragedy and disaster for millions.

4

INSTALLING A KING IN THE NAME OF DEMOCRACY

AND SO, INSTEAD OF HELPING THE Palestinian people, and instead of helping Mossadegh survive and thrive as a bulwark against Communism as Sir Roger suggested, the United States opted for just the opposite course of action. The game plan the United States ran in Iran in 1953 was the standard one it ran during the Cold War—that is, target a nationalist government for overthrow in the interest of preserving US economic domination, and justify such an overthrow by manufacturing a Communist threat. Such a threat is manufactured, as in the case of Iran, by isolating the targeted country economically and politically, starving its economy (or, "making the economy scream" as Henry Kissinger put it in reference to the United States' policy toward Chile's Allende government), and thereby pushing that country into the arms of the Soviets. Then, the United States could claim that it must overthrow that country's government because of its ties to the Soviets—ties that the United States forced upon them.

As for the part of the plan to starve the targeted country's economy, that plan was aggressively followed by the United States and Britain in their goal to topple Mossadegh, and it worked like a charm. Thus, Iran was prevented from receiving any revenue from its oil as a consequence of a worldwide embargo and blockade against Iranian oil which was aggressively enforced by the British Navy. Meanwhile, the United States itself, in support of Britain, refused to buy Iranian oil. The result was that "the country's main source of income was gone. Iran had earned $45 million from oil exports in 1950, more than 70 percent of its total earnings. That sum dropped by half in 1951 and then to almost zero in 1952."[1]

As a May 30, 1953, memorandum of a conversation between the Shah and US Ambassador Loy W. Henderson reflects, even the Shah, the United States' hand-picked successor to Mossadegh and soon-to-be tyrannical dictator, was alarmed at the situation.[2] As the memo relates, "Shah told by Henderson that U.S. would not buy Iranian oil for the foreseeable future unless dispute with Britain was resolved, nor would it give financial or economic aid." It should be noted that, as reflected in the 2017 released documents, the resolution of the oil dispute, at least on the surface, now came down to the question of how much Iran would pay Great Britain as compensation for the nationalization of the oil fields.[3]

The Shah gave his opinion that the best chance for settlement was under Mossadegh rather than a successor, and he further "said that the present economic position of Iran is so dangerous that he would like to see the U.S. give financial and economic assistance to the country even though Dr. Mossadegh was still in power and even though the extension of that assistance might make it appear that the U.S. was supporting Mossadegh."[4]

The United States was unmoved by the Shah's plea. As a later, June 19, 1953, memorandum of conversation relates, it was agreed by the major US decision-makers, including President Eisenhower himself, that Mossadegh would be told that the United States was refusing to give him any economic aid, as "it would be unfortunate at this time to give Mossadegh any ammunition which would strengthen his political position."[5] The United States even refused economic support to Mossadegh though it knew that the Soviets were offering help, and that this was putting the Soviets in a favorable light in the eyes of the Iranians, while making the United States look bad. Thus, in a paper prepared by the CIA, and dated July 22, 1953, the CIA notes that "Soviet action in making about $21,000,000 available lends itself a contrast to American failure to grant financial aid."[6]

The United States even rebuffed what appeared to be an incredible offer by Mossadegh. Thus, a May 4, 1953, telegram from the US Embassy in Iran to the Department of State quotes Mossadegh as stating, "I am willing have this dispute settled by someone whom Britain and I can trust. I agreeable President Eisenhower act as arbiter. I ready give him full power to decide issue. Will you be good enough to ask President Eisenhower if he would undertake settle this matter for us?"[7] A June 19 memo relates that "it is agreed that no response should be given to Mosadeq in regard to his request that Eisenhower settle the dispute."[8] Instead, silence would be the rude reply to Mossadegh's incredibly conciliatory proposal, and Mossadegh and the Iranian people in general would soon learn never to put their trust in an American president again.

One might ask at this point what was going on here. If Mossadegh's rule did not really pose a risk of Communist takeover of Iran, with the British ambassador even opining that Mossadegh might represent the best bulwark against Communism; and if, as the Shah believed, Mossadegh offered the best possibility for settling the oil dispute with Britain, with Mossadegh even offering for Eisenhower to be the sole arbiter of that dispute, then why did the United States believe that it had to forcibly remove Mossadegh?

I believe the answer is twofold: (1) the United States, as has been its wont certainly since WWII, felt the need to punish Mossadegh and Iran for attempting to nationalize Iran's oil to begin with; in short, as Noam Chomsky has often explained, the United States would have to wipe out the "danger of a good example" to other upstart nations who might get similar ideas; and (2) the United States now saw an opportunity to muscle in to the Iranian oil market itself, and to at least partially displace Britain in this respect.

What the evidence strongly shows, despite a number of allusions in the released documents to the alleged need to protect Iranian democracy, is that the advancement of democracy and freedom was certainly NOT part of the US program for Iran. Thus, in addition to the obvious threats to democracy posed by the forcible installation of a royal monarch in power, along with the installation of a Nazi sympathizer as prime minister, the released documents evidence a complete contempt for the will of the Iranian people and the resolve to use brutality to suppress that will. And, as time went on, the United States' support for brutal repression in Iran only increased.

So, for example, in a memo to US Ambassador Henderson, dated May 19, 1953, the counselor of embassy, Mattison, gives his quite reasonable opinion that while forcing a change of government in Iran might lead to the United States obtaining the ends it wanted, the resulting regime "would probably take the form of a military dictatorship or a dictatorship supported by the military, as there is some doubt that sufficient popular support could be obtained for a settlement on British terms."[9] History would of course prove Mattison correct in this regard.

The fact was that, as US policymakers would often acknowledge in their internal documents, Mossadegh, despite the problems he was facing—problems largely created by the conscious work of the United Kingdom and United States to sink the Iranian economy—was still popular and still the single most important politician in Iran. Thus, in a May 8, 1953, telegram from the US Embassy to the State Department, Ambassador Henderson opines that "Mosadeq still however, outstanding political figure [in] Iran."[10]

In a July 1, 1953, "Despatch from the Embassy in Iran to the Department of State," the first secretary of the embassy actually pays tribute to Mossadegh, stating:

> There seems to be no question of the broad base of popular support for
> Dr. Mosadeq at the time he first took office as Prime Minister. As leader
> of the struggle against the Anglo-Iranian Oil Company in a country

where resentment and even hatred of the British is deep-rooted, Mosadeq could count upon the support of people from all levels of society with but few exceptions. For many months after the oil nationalization, the Prime Minister's popularity continually mounted. To the common people, Mosadeq was looked upon almost as a demigod.

The phenomenon of Mosadeq was almost unique in Iran. The figure of a frail, old man, in an Oriental country where age of itself commands respect, who appeared to be successfully winning a battle against remarkable odds, aroused the sympathy of all Iranians. In a country where political corruption had been the accepted norm, there now appeared a man whose patriotism and financial honesty were unassailable.[11]

Here, the embassy paints the picture of a man of great, and indeed unique, virtue. But this Despatch is written in a way as to blame the victim—Mossadegh—for the problems that would beset him—particularly the economic ones which were bringing Mossadegh's government to the brink of ruin. Thus, the Despatch states that Mossadegh's standing with the people changed due to the worsening of the economic and financial situation of the country. What the memo doesn't acknowledge, however, is how Great Britain, with the full support of the United States, intentionally wrecked Iran's economy under Mossadegh in order to bring about his demise. And, a key to this economic warfare, of course, was Britain's sabotage against Iran's oil industry and the worldwide embargo against Iranian oil which the UK enforced using the British Navy.

Elsewhere though, clearly acknowledging the fatal harm intentionally being done to the Iranian economy for the past couple of years, another, undated memorandum states the following: "Recognizing that the economic and political stability of Iran is to a large degree dependent on the revival of its chief industry, both the US and UK will take appropriate steps to encourage and facilitate the resumption of large-scale exports of Iranian oil" after Mossadegh was gone.[12] That is, the United States recognized what would bring stability to the Iranian government; it just wouldn't do what was necessary until Mossadegh was gone and the United States' chosen government was installed.

And still, even as the appointed hour for the coup approached, the CIA was forced to acknowledge Mossadegh's enduring popularity with the people. Thus, in another July 1953 memo, the CIA concludes that Mossadegh would "receive overwhelming popular support" for his planned referendum on dissolution of present Majlis and "revocation of the Shah's power to appoint prime minister by royal firman."[13] That is, the CIA realized that Mossadegh had the support of the people and that the Shah did not, but the plan to replace Mossadegh with the rule of the Shah had to proceed.

Then again, in a July 8, 1953, memo, Kermit Roosevelt cites a trusted Iranian source, in an "estimate of Mossadegh's strength," saying the following:

> "(1) Mossadegh is the only strong political figure in Iran.
> (2) Mossadegh has the confidence of all people except a few disgruntled aristocrats.
> Mossadegh cannot be ousted at this time."[14]

Recognizing Mossadegh's popularity amongst the people, and still bent upon getting rid of him just the same, the CIA proceeded with its plan on forcing him out. And so, just about two weeks after the previous memo assessing Mossadegh's formidable strength as a political figure in Iran was sent, the CIA, by memo dated July 22, 1953, set forth its list of people to arrest on the night of the coup.

And, of course, the list included Mossadegh himself, amongst many others:

> "A. Arrest list:
> (1) To be arrested night of coup: Mossadegh, Riahi, Ashrafi, Modaber Rasavi, Hassibi, Shayegan, Zirakezadeh, Sanjabi, Khalil

Maleki, Forouar of Pan Iran, Amini of Gendarmerie, Sareshteh of M.P.

(2) Sixty members Tudeh

(3) Eventually if disturbances occur 300 other individuals have to be jailed or placed under house arrest."[15]

Memos such as this show just how much control the CIA had over every detail of the coup. This was in fact a coup Made in America, and it would be the first of many such coups that the CIA would engineer over the years to come.

Some of these documents are downright creepy, not only setting forth "arrest lists," but also suggesting the need for mass murder. But before getting into what is written, it must be noted what is not written, for there is still much listed as "not declassified" in these CIA documents, and this information is almost invariably under the most tantalizing headings, such as "Political and Psychological Warfare," "Paramilitary Operations," "Political Assets," "Military Assets," "Religious Assets," and my personal favorite, "Penetration Assets."

But what is written is frightening enough. For example, in a July 30, 1953, CIA memo, there is a paragraph entitled, "Roosevelt/Station Recommendation to Solve Qashqai/Amini Problem."[16] The Qashqai is a pastoral clan made up of a number of tribes living mostly in the Fars region of Iran, at that time numbering in the tens of thousands, and they are often mentioned in the memos as a "problem" for the CIA and Roosevelt because of their strong support for Mossadegh. The Amini appears to be a reference to the family of Ali Amini, who was then serving in the cabinet of Mossadegh, and again posed a challenge to Operation AJAX, or TPAJAX as the CIA called it.

Roosevelt's recommendation for these folks was short, but not so sweet: "Proceed with TPAJAX and attempt to enlist under most favorable circumstances cooperation of certain elements of Qashqais/Aminis. If cooperation cannot be gained they should be neutralized. This should be done in such a way as to eliminate danger premature exposure of TPAJAX." Just a few months before, in a March 1 memo from the CIA to President Eisenhower, the Qashqai had been described as a CIA asset to whom the CIA was planning to give small arms, ammunition, and cash to resist a potential Communist take-over.[17] Now, they were a problem to be "neutralized."

The term "neutralize" in CIA parlance can definitely denote physical extermination, and that appears to be the case here, especially given future events and given the person of Kermit Roosevelt who, at one point in the documents, jokingly criticizes the Shah for having "old-fashioned ideas against assassination." Roosevelt would not have to wait too long, however, for the Shah to get over his "old-fashioned" sensibilities, for he would very soon embrace the ideas of torture and murder with great élan.

In addition, while the Qashqai were originally compliant with the coup government in August of 1953, they were cowed into submission by Brigadier Davalu who, as indicated in an August 21, 1953, note in the newly-released CIA documents, warns that if the Qashqai rebel against the new regime, they "will promptly and mercilessly be wiped out by air and land."[18] In other words, a genocide of these people was being threatened.

And, as recorded in an August 28, 1953, memo of what looks like a huge meeting of the CIA, Roosevelt again states that "fairly drastic action" must be taken with the Qashqai clan if they don't support the Shah, and how, with respect to the four brothers in charge of the clan, "the time has come for them to go."[19] Everyone in the room knows what this means as judged by the remark of Richard Helms—by then a longtime veteran of the CIA and its OSS predecessor, and later to become the director of the CIA and then ambassador to Iran. Thus, Helms quips, "When this fellow Roosevelt says somebody has got to go, you sort of go like this, don't you, or they have had it?" The next three and a half lines of dialogue, which includes two lines of remarks by Roosevelt himself, are listed as "not declassified."

Later in this same meeting, Roosevelt states quite explicitly how he believed that Mossadegh's chief of staff of the armed forces, General Taghi Riahi, "should be executed" for his lack of loyalty to the Shah and his key role in foiling the initial coup attempt against Mossadegh.

We would learn a little about General Riahi through an interview he had with US General McClure at the US Embassy shortly after the first failed coup attempt—an interview summarized in a telegram from the embassy dated August 16, 1953.[20] In this interview, he explained how most of the military was still loyal to Mossadegh, how the "Army would support people," and how, under Mossadegh, "Iran had adopted policy of long range benefit to its people; that Iran wanted and needed sympathetic help of free world particularly US but that she would not deviate from that policy even though it meant loss of aid and even friendship of US. He repeated his desire for continued help." A man of principles like this, as Mossadegh was as well, simply could not be tolerated by Roosevelt and his ilk and therefore had to be eliminated.

In the above, we witness what Hannah Arendt, in describing the crimes of Nazi Adolf Eichmann, termed, "the banality of evil"—that is, the commission of monstrous deeds by seemingly normal people in an environment in which evil has become so routine as to appear normal.

The CIA had created such an environment even back then, and it was an environment in which neatly-groomed, well-dressed, and spectacled killers like Kermit Roosevelt thrived.

Richard Helms, described by one writer as "the gentlemanly planner of assassinations," was another who thrived in the CIA system.[21] Helms himself would later be involved in plots to kill Fidel Castro and in the successful plot to kidnap Chilean General Renee Schneider—a kidnapping plot which resulted in Schneider's being killed and which paved the way for the overthrow of President Salvador Allende.

In addition, it was Helms who, at this very time, in April 1953, proposed to Allen Dulles the idea of what became the CIA's infamous

MK-Ultra Program, a program for the covert use of biological and chemical agents for purposes of mind control, psychological operations, torture, and political assassination.[22] Ex-Nazis were used to help develop this program under a madman known as CIA operative Sidney Gottlieb, an individual some say "personified [the] CIA's immoral universe" and who became the inspiration for Dr. Strangelove.[23] This program, which was developed through testing on unsuspecting Americans and Canadians, some of whom lost their minds and their lives as a result,[24] was officially discontinued in 1976 as the Senate, led by Senator Frank Church, began to investigate the misdeeds of the CIA. Helms, then CIA chief, ordered all of the files of this program destroyed to shield the information from the investigation.

Ultimately, the neutralization of the Qashqai clan did come as warned. In 1967, after a five-year revolt against the Shah, the Qashqai clan rebellion was finally put down through aerial bombardment, with the Iranian military using two squadrons of US F-4 fighter-bombers.[25]

Meanwhile, the CIA explains that, once the coup against Mossadegh succeeds, "the U.S. government should confine any comment upon a change in government in Iran to a repetition of our traditional unwillingness to interfere in the internal affairs of a free country and our willingness to work with the government in power. . . . The U.S. Government should avoid any statement that the oil question is involved in a change of government in Iran."[26] In other words, the United States should lie as usual about its true intentions in overturning a foreign government.

The United States' serial lying about foreign intervention is actually raised in these documents in a quite humorous exchange between a member of the Iranian Majlis, Dr. Mozaffar Baqai, and US Ambassador Loy W. Henderson. In this conversation, which takes place shortly after the coup and as the new Iranian government is preparing to settle the oil dispute on terms favorable to Britain and the United States, Dr. Baqai says, with what appears to be complete sincerity, "that when the United States decided for reasons of political or military necessity to intervene in Korea it had had to profess high-sounding and possibly fictitious reasons for its actions; in the same manner, the Iranian government could not be completely frank with its people as to the necessity and reasons behind an oil settlement."[27]

In the face of such obvious truth, Ambassador Henderson is said to have taken "sharp issue" with Dr. Baqai, claiming that "the United States had acted solely in order to resist Communist aggression and to keep its word to the free world." Of course, this is not the case at all. Thus, while the United States claimed, and continues to claim, that it intervened in 1950 in response to the "invasion" by North Korea of South Korea, this ignores the fact that the United States had already been intervening in Korea since 1945, helping the government in South Korea, which had collaborated with fascist Japan, to jail and kill leftists and nationalists who had resisted Japanese occupation.

All told, 100,000 such dissidents, though true patriots, were killed by the South Korean government, with US backing, before 1950.[28] And, during the course of the Korean War, the US military would go on to level nearly every building in North Korea and every one of its dams necessary for food cultivation, engage in rape of Korean women on a mass scale, and kill around 3 million North Koreans. I guess this is what is meant by keeping our "word to the free world."

Moreover, the idea that North Korea's crossing the artificially-drawn thirty-eighth parallel—a line drawn arbitrarily by two US generals as WWII was ending—could be the business of any other country is just silly, given that Korea had been a unified country for the two thousand years prior.[29] This would be like another country intervening in the United States because the North had crossed the Mason-Dixon line and "invaded" the South during the Civil War and had even gone so far as to burn Atlanta down to the ground in the process. Dr. Baqai was indeed no fool, knowing full well of the United States' dissembling and hypocrisy in such matters.

In any case, back to the US intervention against the Mossadegh government. Early on, as initial preparations are being made for the overthrow, the CIA lays out a list of its assets which it has had in Iran for some time, even before the coup plans had been formulated and green-lighted by Eisenhower.

Again, while many of the descriptions of these assets remains "not declassified," the ones now declassified, and set forth in a March 3, 1953, CIA memo, include: "*Mass Propaganda means* (press, etc.): CIA controls a network with numerous press, political, and clerical contacts which has proven itself capable of disseminating large-scale . . . propaganda . . . ; *Poison Pen, personal denunciations, rumor spreading, etc.:* CIA has means of making fairly effective personal attacks against any political figure in Iran, including Mossadegh. . . . ; *Street Riots, demonstrations, mobs, etc.:* CIA *[less than 1 line not declassified]*. . . . The CIA also explains that it "has one group in Iran which, it is believed, may be fairly effective in carrying on morale sabotage within the country and stimulating various types of small scale resistance."[30]

Similarly, in another CIA memo, dated April 16, 1953, the CIA, under a heading entitled, "Activist Assets," discusses the fact that "[less than 1 line not declassified] have the capabilities of bringing out gangs of street fighters. Through *[less than 1 line not declassified]* contacts with leaders of various segments of the Pan-Iranists they have encouraged this group to engage in street fights with the Tudeh Party. . . ."[31]

And, of course, the CIA had stockpiles of readily-available cash and weapons. Thus, in a March 20, 1953 progress report to the National Security Council, the CIA explains that "[a]t the present the CIA has a stockpile of small arms, ammunition and demolition materiel *[less than 1 line not declassified]*. The stockpile is in quantity designed to supply a 10,000-man guerilla force for six months without resupply. . . ."[32]

As one author puts it succinctly, the CIA's "agents in Tehran bought off secular politicians, religious leaders and key military officers. They hired thugs to run rampant through the street, sometimes pretending to be Mossadegh supporters, sometimes calling for his overthrow, anything to create a chaotic political situation. Money was spread around the offices of newspaper editors and radio station owners as well."[33]

The plan was to create chaos and confusion which would be blamed on Mossadegh, and then to move against Mossadegh by arresting him at his home in the middle of the night. The plan was to happen as follows, as a CIA memo of July 22, 1953, lays out:

Re arrest Mossadegh: Zahedi plan as follows:

(1) Block where his house located to be surrounded by Palace Guard.
(2) Col Daftari and Capt. Davar Panah who in charge Mossadegh person guard are "in hand" Zahedi and at his bidding will apprehend Mossadegh and deliver him to Zahedi.
(3) Mossadegh will then be taken custody in village outside Tehe [Tehran].
(4) Rumor will be circulated Mossadegh dead. This for purpose of causing followers lose hope and rally other banner presumably Zahedi.[34]

The memo goes on to say that "all premises used by political groups [are] to be closed" after the coup.

As indicated above, the first attempt at this plan did not succeed because Mossadegh's chief of staff, General Riahi, who was marked as someone who should be arrested as well on the night of the coup and who Roosevelt then wanted killed, got wise to the plan in time and took precautions to protect Mossadegh. The coup, at this point, looked doomed, with a CIA memo dated August 17, 1953, concluding: "Except in the unlikely event that a strong and resolute opposition majority develops in some future Majlis, any future attempt to unseat Mossadegh will necessarily be an out-and-out coup, without legal sanction."[35]

However, the one thing the CIA still had going for it was the fact that few had caught on to the fact that the United States had been behind the attempt. And, it would in fact be Mossadegh's faith in, and kind feelings for, the Americans that would ultimately be his undoing, as we shall soon see.

As an August 16, 1953, telegram from the US Embassy to the Department of State explains, only the communist Tudeh Party's newspaper, *Shojat*, carried any account of the attempted coup whatsoever. However, Tudeh was right on the mark, explaining in the paper that "American imperialists sent [General Norman] Schwarzkopf [yes, the father of "Stormin'" Norman Schwarzkopf of First Gulf War fame] as spy to court after Dulles and Eisenhower statements with instructions present government must be ousted by military action and replaced by government headed by men like Alayar Saleh, General Zahedi, Hakimi, Dr. Amini."[36] Luckily for the CIA, few folks of importance read the communist party paper, and so a second attempt could be made.

And, this attempt was made and succeeded in a most devious way. Thus, while Kermit Roosevelt again set plans into to motion to cause street riots and other provocations, while personally hiding General Zahedi until the right moment, he needed one last ruse to pull off Operation AJAX. There is a reference to this in the CIA documents when Ambassador Henderson, in a telegram to the US State Department, explains how he went to see Mossadegh at his home. He then told the unsuspecting Mossadegh that he was "particularly concerned [about] increasing attacks on Americans," and how every hour or two he was "receiving additional reports [of] attacks on American citizens not only in Tehran but also other localities."[37] He pleaded with Mossadegh to call on law enforcement agencies to take affirmative action to protect Americans.

What is not said here is that Henderson was meeting with Mossadegh as part of Roosevelt's plans to create enough pressure to blow the lid off the situation on the streets of Tehran. The problem, as Stephen

Kinzer explains so well in his great book *All The Shah's Men*, was that Mossadegh was too restrained in the face of the terrible violence being stoked by the CIA.

As Kinzer relates:

> The riots that shook Tehran on Monday intensified on Tuesday. Thousands of demonstrators, unwittingly under CIA control, surged through the streets, looting shops, destroying pictures of the Shah, and ransacking the offices of royalist groups. Exuberant nationalists and communists joined in the mayhem. The police were still under orders from Mossadegh not to interfere. That allowed rioters to do their jobs, which was to give the impression that Iran was sliding towards anarchy. Roosevelt caught glimpses of them during his furtive trips around the city and said that they 'scared the hell out of him.'

The riots were working to a point, but now Roosevelt needed an over-reaction by Mossadegh to justify what amounted to a military coup in the name of restoring order and democracy. This is where Ambassador Henderson comes in. Thus, as Kinzer explains, Henderson was told by Roosevelt to go to Mossadegh and to ask him for police to crack down on the rioters in Tehran in order to protect the lives of Americans who were allegedly under threat and attack.

In so doing, Roosevelt and Henderson were appealing to Mossadegh's better angels to undo him. As Kinzer puts it, "Roosevelt had perfectly analyzed his adversary's psyche. Mossadegh, steeped in a culture of courtliness and hospitality, found it shocking that guests in Iran were being mistreated. That shock overwhelmed his good judgment, and with Henderson still in the room, he picked up a telephone and called his police chief. Trouble in the streets had become intolerable, he said, and it was time for the police to put an end to it. With this order, Mossadegh sent the police out to attack a mob that included many of his own most fervent supporters."

The fuse had been lit, and Roosevelt was ecstatic. As he wrote in a "Telegram From the Station in Iran to the Central Intelligence Agency," dated August 19, 1953, "Overthrow of Mossadegh appears on verge of success. Zahedi now at radio station."[38] Roosevelt then requested emergency economic aid for the new government after having starved out Mossadegh's government, asking "urgently that 5 million dollars be held immediately available to support new govt and enable it to meet payroll."

By August 20, 1953, the coup had been successful, with Mossadegh's home being stormed and looted, and with Mossadegh taken away under arrest. The Shah was then summoned back from his own self-imposed exile at the time prescribed by Kermit Roosevelt. As planned, the Shah's monarchy was fully restored and General Zahedi was installed as prime minister in Mossadegh's stead.

As another telegram from Roosevelt, dated August 20, 1953, rejoiced: "Complete (new government) lineup now appointed. Momtaz had to be killed. Will keep you advised."[39] Here, Roosevelt was (quite matter-of-factly) referring to Mossadegh loyalist Colonel Anatollo of Momtaz who was killed attempting to protect Mossadegh.

In a record of a meeting of the CIA, dated August 28, 1953,[40] a proud and boastful Kermit Roosevelt relates the story of how the coup proceeded. For one, he explains with glee how the Tudeh members were mistreated—i.e., how the Army "beat the hell out of them, and they carted away four truckloads of bloody Tudeh." He further relates how he was promised by both the Shah and General Zahedi "that very vigorous measures would be taken" against the Tudeh—at the time of the coup, a legal political party, by the way. It is also here where Roosevelt expresses his belief that "fairly drastic action" must be taken with the Qashqai Clan, and how he told the Shah that he believed that General Riahi should be executed.

The coup government now installed, though still precariously, any pretenses to such lofty goals as democracy and freedom were quickly abandoned. First of all, though one might believe that the CIA's work was done, it had in fact just begun, with the Directorate of Plans for the CIA explaining in an August 1953 memo that the coup had "created a favorable atmosphere for CIA operations in the country."[41] He also reiterates here how "the new government wasted no time in clamping down on the Tudeh Party by raiding cells and publications and making arrests." We learn in an undated briefing note for the CIA director that in fact 1300 Tudeh members were arrested in short order after the coup.[42]

In a "Monthly Report Prepared in the Directorate of Plans, CIA," dated September 1953, it is mentioned how General Zahedi's government was now firmly established in light of $45 million in emergency funds sent to him by the United States.[43] Meanwhile, the CIA relates how the "Shah feels that the Majlis should not be brought into session because a strong authoritarian government is necessary to provide the country's internal stability." Further, "The Shah . . . has issued orders that Mossadegh be killed immediately by his guards in case of any serious Tudeh rebellion." And again, it is explained that "CIA capabilities have become greatly enhanced both in terms of short-term political action programs designed to support the existing government and in terms of long-range programs designed to promote the internal stability, general welfare, and strong western orientation of the country."

On October 23, 1953, in a "Memorandum of Conversation," it is noted by the CIA, without too much concern, that "of the 4,000 persons imprisoned as suspected Communists, some 30 percent [or well over 1000] are entirely innocent."[44] And, "the remainder" are "only rank and file members" or "sympathizers." Of course, given how the CIA is defining "guilt" and "innocence" here, with someone being "guilty" if they were merely members of the hitherto legal Tudeh Party, the percentage of "innocent" behind bars was most likely much higher than 30 percent of the 4,000 persons imprisoned. This type of mass and disproportionate political repression was all according to plan, with the CIA Directorate of Plans explaining on October 29, 1953, that "through U.S. advice and good offices, the Iranian government is being encouraged in taking a firm stand against the opposition and is conducting an intensive drive against the Tudeh."[45]

Things continued to move quickly toward a more repressive system in Iran, and seemingly with US approval. For example, in a dispatch dated November 13, 1953, Roosevelt speaks openly about how prior Iranian elections were manipulated and stolen through tactics such as ballot stuffing and false vote tallying, and that the CIA would have to "resort to the same methods, through the government and the Shah for the election of a Majlis favorable to our purposes in Iran."[46]

An editorial note in the newly-released documents then explains: "In a memorandum to Secretary of State Dulles, July 30, 1954, Acting Special Assistant for Intelligence Fisher Howe discussed the political prospects for Iran. He wrote that political power in Iran was exercised by the Shah and the landowning classes. . . . Iran's power structure was maintained by the continuance of martial law, the enforcement of strict press censorship, the work of the security forces, the provision of U.S. emergency aid, and the expectation of an oil settlement in favor of Iran."[47]

Similarly, a National Intelligence Estimate dated December 7, 1954, explains that "the principal new features of the present power situation are: (a) the extensive use of authoritarian means—martial law, censorship, and prosecution or repression of opponents—to curtail opposition to the regime and the government. . . ." The estimate goes on to state that "so long as Zahedi is Prime Minister, the government will almost certainly continue a fairly firm policy of repression."[48]

Again, there is no hint here that the coup government had any plans on democratizing Iran, or that the United States had any such intentions either.

Meanwhile, in a November 5, 1953, dispatch from the US Embassy to the US State Department, we see the logical result of the US collaboration with Nazi sympathizers. And, apparently, like father, like son, the new Shah, who would dub himself "Light of the Aryans,"[49] was one such sympathizer. Thus, the embassy, again without any apparent concern, explains that "the Shah and his administration are encouraging the growth of quasi-military and fascist-type groups as added insurance against the possibility of further Tudeh mob actions."[50]

And, under the heading, *"Anti-Tudeh Organizations,"* the embassy explains, "There are indications that within recent weeks the Shah and the Government have been encouraging the growth of quasi-military rightist parties to be used against the Tudeh in the event of further demonstrations. . . . These organizations . . . have all the trappings of a falange or fascist type of group, even to their black-shirted uniforms. The Sumka demonstrated its strength and discipline on the occasion of the recent Sports Festival, when approximately 500 of its members impressed the crowds at the Stadium with a show of swastika-bedecked banners carried in perfect marching order. These organizations . . . almost certainly receive their excellent financial backing from the Shah and the administration."

Black shirts with "swastika-bedecked banners" marching in Tehran. Mission accomplished! Again, if this seems surprising, one needs to look not only to history, but also to current events to see other examples of the United States happily working with the worst groups, including Nazis, to obtain its goals. Again, throughout the Cold War, the United States invariably sided with fascist and even neo-Nazi regimes as a bulwark against Communism, socialism, and even just liberalism, and the United States continues to side with such elements when it suits its sometime-hard-to-discern interests.

One example during the Cold War was in Chile where the United States helped to overthrow socialist President Dr. Salvador Allende in a coup which closely resembled the coup against Mossadegh and which brought to power the fascist Pinochet regime. The nadir of Pinochet's reign was the bizarre state-within-a-state, Colonia

Dignidad, a fascist German colony founded by Paul Schaeffer, a Nazi and former medic of the Nazi's Luftwaffe.[51] Colonia Dignidad became a "clandestine detention and torture center" for the Pinochet regime. As one victim of the Colonia's torture explains, "Right after the coup, the Chilean military didn't know how to torture. . . . People would die very quickly. Germans in the colony knew how to keep a person alive for several days or weeks while putting him through the most terrible agony and humiliation."[52]

The Iranians were also novices in modern torture techniques, and so, as we shall soon see, after the coup against Mossadegh, the CIA helped train the Iranian security services in torture techniques—techniques borrowed, as in the case of Pinochet's Chile, from the experts on such subjects -- the Nazis.

And again, this type of alliance is not a thing of the past. The best example of this today is in Ukraine where, as Max Blumenthal writes, "Massive torchlit rallies pour out into the streets of Kiev on regular occasions, showcasing columns of Azov members rallying beneath the Nazi-inspired Wolfsangel banner that serves as the militia's symbol."[53] As Blumenthal explains, Azov is a militia now incorporated into the Ukranian National Guard, and, despite its openly pro-Nazi ideology, including violent anti-Semitism, this militia has obtained heavy US weaponry transfers "right under the nose of the US State Department," while "U.S. trainers and U.S. volunteers have been working closely with this battalion."

The former left-wing president of Uruguay, Jose Mujica, who was known as the "poorest president in the world," has been quoted as saying that it is not even fair to call the Azvov militiamen "neo-Nazis" because they are in fact true Nazis, tracing their roots, and quite proudly, back to WWII. As Blumenthal explains, they trace their history back to the Nazi collaborationist militia known as the Organization of Ukrainian Nationalists (OUN) which worked alongside German troops in fighting the Soviet Union and in committing pogroms against Ukrainian Jews, with one pogrom alone killing seven thousand Jews.

Not surprisingly, the CIA began working with the (OUN) right after the war in attempting to counter the Soviet Union, and the United States has been working with the OUN and its successor groups ever since.

It should come as no surprise then, that the United States would work with Nazi sympathizers in Iran, or that the CIA would go on to train Iran's security services in Nazi torture techniques. And this is indeed just what happened.

Meanwhile, the United Kingdom and the United States both got what they wanted all along with the fall of Mossadegh. Thus, the Anglo Iranian Oil Company was reorganized into British Petroleum, or BP for short.[54] And, according to an appendix in the newly-released CIA documents, it received 40 percent of the Iranian oil industry. The United States received another 40 percent of the industry, split between five companies—according to the appendix, Gulf-International Company (8 percent), Standard Oil Company of California (now, Chevron) (8 percent), Standard Oil of New Jersey (now, ExxonMobil) (8 percent), Texas Company (now, a subsidiary of Chevron) (8 percent), and Socony-Vacuum Overseas Supply Company (now, ExxonMobil) (8 percent). An additional 14 percent of Iran's industry went to Royal Dutch Shell, with the remaining 4 percent to a French company.[55]

For his grand prize, Kermit Roosevelt would become Vice-President of Gulf Oil, a quite natural next job for the man who helped make Iran safe for Western oil companies, including Gulf itself. To his credit, though, he left the CIA for a job at Gulf because, while forever proud of his coup orchestration in Iran, he was not interested in going along with the Dulles brothers' next coup in Guatemala in 1954.[56] Roosevelt was rightly fearful that the CIA would get too used to overthrowing foreign governments, many times against the will of the people, and he did not believe that this was a prudent or ethical idea.[57]

As for President Eisenhower, he seemed to be less than proud of what the United States had done in Iran. Thus, an October 8, 1953, entry in his diary which is quoted in the newly-released documents about the coup reads: "Another recent development that we helped bring about was the restoration of the Shah to power in Iran and the elimination of Mossadegh. The things we did were 'covert.' If knowledge of them became public, we would not only be embarrassed in the region, but our chances to do anything of like nature in the future would totally disappear."[58] Of course, Eisenhower would not let much time go by before he was involved in another coup of "like nature" in Guatemala, with possibly even more disastrous results.

5

THE CIA AND THE SAVAK

The Eisenhower-Dulles era was a Pax Americana enforced by terror.
The administration ensured U.S. postwar global dominance by
threatening enemies with nuclear annihilation or with coups and
assassinations. It was empire on the cheap, a product of
Ike's desire to avoid another large-scale shooting war as well as the
imperial burdens that had bankrupted Great Britain.
—David Talbot, *The Devil's Chessboard*

EVER SINCE THE SHAH—"OUR BOY," AS Kermit Roosevelt referred to him—was overthrown in 1979, the United States has been relentlessly involved in attempts at regime change in Iran. These attempts continue to this day, with a number of US leaders openly talking about the need to oust the Islamic government.

In 2017, the United States spent over $1 million in financing anti-government protests in Iran and in trying to convert spontaneous protests into a push for regime change, and another $20 million on Voice of America's Persian Service which is also aimed at turning Iranian public opinion against the government.[1] And since 2006, successive US administrations have sought "to exploit these crises [e.g., economic, water, and energy crises] to undermine the legitimacy of the regime, by funding opposition groups as well as anti-regime broad-casting to the tune of tens of millions of dollars a year."

As Mint Press notes, "Much of the media programming funded by the State Department has focused on glorifying the reign of the Shah of Iran. . . . The propaganda appears to have worked, with many participants in the latest protests calling for the Shah's exiled son, Reza Pahlavi, to return to power in Iran."[2]

Especially given that the United States views the restoration of the Shah as a possible option for Iran and given that the State Department is busy spending our tax dollars in trying to convince Iranians how great the rule of the Shah was before his overthrow, it is worth looking at this claim.

For many Iranians, the nature of the Shah's reign is best typified by his infamous security apparatus known as the SAVAK. The nature of the SAVAK, moreover, says much about the nature of the foreign policy of the United States which helped to create it and support it for over twenty years.

A great, succinct summary of the SAVAK, and the US relationship with it, can be found in Dean Henderson's *Big Oil & Their Bankers in The Persian Gulf*:

> Wherever the Four Horsemen (Exxon Mobil, Chevron Texaco, BP Amoco & Royal Dutch/Shell) gallop the CIA is close behind. Iran was no exception. By 1957 the Company, as intelligence insiders know the CIA, created one of its first Frankensteins—the Shah of Iran's brutal secret police known as SAVAK.
>
> Kermit Roosevelt, the Mossadegh *coup*-master turned Northrop salesman, admitted in his memoirs that SAVAK was 100% created by the CIA and Mossad, the Israeli intelligence agency that acts as appendage of the CIA. For the next 20 years the CIA and SAVAK were joined at the hip when it came to matters of Persian Gulf security.

Three hundred fifty SAVAK agents were shuttled each year to CIA training facilities in McLean, Virginia, where they learned the finer arts of interrogation and torture. Top SAVAK brass were trained through the US Agency for International Development's (USAID) Public Safety Program, until it was shut down in 1973 due to its reputation for turning out some of the world's finest terrorists. . . .

Popular anger towards Big Oil, the Shah and his new police state resulted in mass protests. The Shah dealt with the peaceful demonstrations with sheer brutality and got a wink and nod from Langley. From 1957-79 Iran housed 125,000 political prisoners. SAVAK "disappeared" dissenters, a strategy replicated by CIA surrogate dictators in Argentina and Chile.

. . . In 1974 the director of Amnesty International declared that no country had a worse human rights record than Iran. The CIA responded by increasing its support for SAVAK.[3]

For its part, the *Washington Post*, in an article written shortly after the Islamic Revolution, acknowledges that "the CIA 'definitely' trained SAVAK agents in 'both physical and psychological' torture techniques. . . ."[4] The article explained that there were "joint activities" between the SAVAK and the CIA and Israel's Mossad, and that "the Israelis even wrote SAVAK's manuals . . . and prepared an ill-fated effort . . . to undermine the growing religious impact of the revolution."

Well-trained by the CIA, the "Savak—*Sazman-i Etelaat va Amniyat-I Keshvar*, the "National Information and Security Organization"—was to become the most notorious and murderous [of the Shah's security services], its torture chambers among the Middle East's most terrible institutions."[5]

The relationship between the United States and the SAVAK remained close. Indeed "a permanent secret U.S. mission was attached to Savak headquarters. . . ."[6] In addition, Hassan Sana, who had worked for the

SAVAK, spoke after the revolution "of how Savak agents were flown to New York by the CIA for lessons in interrogation techniques at a secret American military base, a mysterious journey that took four hours flying across the United States in an aircraft with darkened windows."[7]

The SAVAK was the original incubator used by the CIA to develop its torture techniques for world-wide distribution. One grisly example of this was illustrated by Mohamed Heikal, one of the "greatest Egyptian journalists, . . . [who] described how Savak filmed the torture of a young Iranian woman, how she was stripped naked and how cigarettes were then used to burn her nipples. According to Heikal, the film was later distributed by the CIA to other intelligence agencies working for American-supported regimes around the world including Taiwan, Indonesia and the Philippines."[8]

Meanwhile, it appears that the SAVAK was at the disposal of US corporations doing business in Iran and wanting some muscle to deal with their workforce. For example, an April 28, 1976, State Department cable (released on Wikileaks), details a messy strike which US tiremaker B.F. Goodrich was having in Iran. As the cable notes, "GOODRICH'S MANAGEMENT HAS MET WITH THE MINISTRY AND WITH SAVAK ON A NUMBER OF OCCASION (sic.) IN AN EFFORT TO GET THE WORKERS BACK ON THE JOB . . ."[9] I imagine the SAVAK could be very persuasive indeed in such matters.

The techniques used by the SAVAK, many borrowed from the Nazis and then passed along to the SAVAK by the CIA,[10] were uniquely grisly and terrible. The SAVAK operated much like the Gestapo, entering a person's home at night, hauling the person away and many times disappearing that person forever. A quite ominous State Department cable (from Wikileaks), dated March 7, 1975, describes such an event:

NYMAN INFORMS THAT WHEN ARRESTED MAJID WAS AT HIS FAMILY HOME IN TEHRAN (118 AVENUE GHAANI— FORMERLY TIR). HIS FATHER HADI GHAVAM INFORMED DAUGHTER (MRS. NYMAN) THAT FIVE SAVAK MEN

ENTERED HOME AT 10 P.M. AND TOOK AWAY MAJID AND
FOUR OF HIS BOOKS. HE HAS NOT BEEN HEARD FROM
SINCE. FATHER ALSO SAID FAIRLY LARGE NUMBER OF
KARAJ STUDENTS ARRESTED AROUND SAME TIME.[11]

This is all the cable says. Most likely, Majid was taken to a prison and
tortured, and very well could have died under torture as so many Iranians did at the hands of the SAVAK.

According to Ryszard Kapuscinski, in his wonderful, *Shah of Shahs*,
"The most common instrument discovered in SAVAK quarters was an
electrically heated table called the 'frying pan,' on which the victim
was tied down by his hands and feet. Many died on these tables. Often,
the accused was already raving by the time he entered the torture
chamber—few people could bear the screams they heard while they
waited, and the smell of burning flesh."[12] The *Washington Post*, in an
article written after a tour of a SAVAK torture center just after the 1979
Revolution, explains how witness "Korteza Amini told how his sister
Fath-meh died, age 33, after six months of torture on the heated bed-
springs had reduced her to a paralyzed wreck."[13]

Kapuscinski does explain that some of the SAVAK's torture techniques were ancient and home-grown. As he relates, "technological
progress could not displace medieval methods in this nightmare world.
In Isfahan, people were thrown into huge bags full of cats crazed and
hungry, or among poisonous snakes. Accounts of such horrors, sometimes, of course, propagated by Savak itself, circulated among the
population for years. They were so threatening, and the definition of
an enemy of the state was so loose and arbitrary, that everyone could
imagine ending up in such a torture chamber."[14]

While well known to the Iranians and the SAVAK's CIA handlers,
this torture took place in the shadows for many years, for the Shah
did not allow human rights groups to view his prisons until the late
1970s. Then, the world would learn of the cruelty being inflicted on the
Iranian people.

As Robert Fisk explains, "The Shah was finally persuaded to allow the International Committee of the Red Cross into Iran's prisons in 1977; they were allowed to see more than 3,000 'security detainees'—political prisoners—in eighteen different jails. They recorded that the inmates had been beaten, burned with cigarettes and chemicals, tortured with electrodes, raped, sodomized with bottles and boiling eggs. Interrogators forced electric cables into the uterus of female prisoners. The Red Cross report named 124 prisoners who had died under torture."[15]

The first comprehensive report I could find from Amnesty International on Iran and the SAVAK was a briefing dated November 1976—just as Jimmy "Human Rights" Carter was preparing to take office as president. The "Amnesty International Briefing, Iran, November, 1976" makes for fascinating, if horrifying, reading, and gives one a glimpse into the dark world which the United States played a key role in manufacturing for the Iranian people.

Amnesty International (AI) described Iran as "in theory a constitutional monarchy with a partially elected parliament, but in practice the Shah has supreme authority."[16] As AI explained, "One important instrument of the Shah's authority is the army . . . [and] the other, equally important, is the National Intelligence and Security Organization (SAVAK) which was formed in 1957 'for the purposes of security of the country and prevention of any kind of conspiracy detrimental to public interests. . . .' The head of the SAVAK is appointed by the Shah and wields unlimited power."[17]

AI related that "the suppression of political opposition is carried out by SAVAK with extreme ruthlessness using a system of informers which permeates all levels of Iranian society and which has created an atmosphere of fear remarked on by visitors to Iran and emphasized by opponents of the regime outside the country."[18]

To put a finer point on it, Robert Fisk explains that, at any given time, the SAVAK employed up to 60,000 agents. A WikiLeaks cable I found put this figure of SAVAK agents at 200,000.[19] And in addition to these full-time employees, the SAVAK used countless informants to maintain the reign of the Shah. According to Fisk, "At one point, it was believed that a third of the male population of Iran were in some way involved in Savak, either directly or as occasional paid or black-mailed informants. They included diplomats, civil servants, mullahs, actors, writers, oil executives, workers, peasants, the poor and unem-ployed, a whole society corrupted by power and fear."

With this army of informants, AI explains, academic freedom was greatly suppressed, with "students and university teachers . . . kept under surveillance by the SAVAK." This, combined with severe press censorship, repressed intellectual inquiry, free speech, and even free thought.

A March 19, 1973, cable from the State Department which I discov-ered on WikiLeaks describes one example of the repressive measures used by the SAVAK against students who dared to protest:

LARGEST AND BLOODIEST ENCOUNTER TO DATE TOOK PLACE IN TABRIZ WHERE STUDENTS BEGAN DEMONSTRA-TION OVER TUITION COSTS AND OTHER LOCAL ISSUES. POLICE INTERVENED AND CONFRONTATION ESCALATED INTO THREE DAY MELEE WITH REPORTS OF OVER 200 STUDENTS INJURED, SOME SERIOUSLY. FIGURES FOR STUDENTS KILLED RANGE FROM THREE TO ELEVEN BUT PRECISE NUMBER OF CASUALTIES IS IMPOSSIBLE TO CON-FIRM. POLICE AND SAVAK EVENTUALLY RAIDED ALL CAMPUS DORMITORIES, INCLUDING THOSE OF GIRLS, DROVE ALL STUDENTS FROM CAMPUS AND CLOSED THE UNIVERSITY DOWN FOR REMAINDER OF TERM.[20]

The same cable notes that protests around the country, and the violent response thereto, "FINALLY RESULTED IN THE CLOSURE, TO ONE DEGREE OR ANOTHER, OF NEARLY ALL OF IRAN'S MAJOR CENTERS OF HIGHER [EDUCATION]".

If such an event—that is, all the country's universities being shut down as a government response to student protest—took place in an adversary country like Venezuela or the Islamic Republic of Iran today, this certainly would make the front page of every newspaper and lead to calls for regime change. But given that this happened under the Shah, little attention was paid.

As the foregoing illustrates, Iran under the Shah was a totalitarian state, ruled much like the notorious *Stasis* in Communist East Germany. The United States, at the height of the Cold War, had helped to create a totalitarian state in order to save the world from totalitarianism, or so we have been told. At the same time, while opposing the one-party states of the Eastern Bloc, the United States had no problem with the one-party state instituted by the Shah in 1975.

As AI again explains, "In 1975 the last pretense of political freedom was removed by abolition of the token opposition *Mardom* Party and the introduction of a one-party system with the formation of the *Rastakhiz* (National Resurgence) Party." AI goes on to relate that, upon instituting the new, one-party rule, "the Shah declared that those who refused to support it could either leave the country or go to prison."[21]

AI, explaining that it was difficult to get a handle on exactly how many political prisoners there were at the time, related that there were at least 3,200 political prisoners as admitted to by the deputy director of the SAVAK himself, and possibly 25,000 to 100,000 as claimed by foreign journalists and Iranian exile groups. Those in jail for oppositional activities included "Muslim dissidents, members of ethnic minorities (Kurds, Baluchis, Azerbaijanis, etc.), and Marxists, but the distinction between these groups are often blurred. . . ."[22]

Torture was endemic, and indeed central, to the Shah's reign. As AI reported, "All observers to trials since 1965 have reported allegations of torture. . . . Alleged methods of torture include whipping and beating, electric shocks, the extraction of nails and teeth, boiling water pumped into the rectum, heavy weights hung on the testicles, tying the prisoner to a metal table heated to white heat, inserting a broken bottle into the anus, and rape."[23]

One former prisoner, Reza Baraheni, reported to AI the following:

Not every prisoner goes through the same process, but generally, this is what happens to a prisoner of the first importance. First, he is beaten by several torturers at once, with sticks and clubs. If he doesn't confess, he is hanged upside down and beaten; if this doesn't work, he is raped; and if he still shows signs of resistance, he is given electric shock which turns him into a howling dog; and if he is still obstinate, his nails and sometimes all his teeth are pulled out; and in certain cases, a hot iron rod is put into one side of the face to force its way to the other side, burning his entire mouth and tongue. A young man was killed this way. . . .[24]

And the United States, while trying to claim at times that it was unaware of the depths of depravity of the SAVAK, was quite aware in real time what it was up to. As one example, a State Department cable from December 5, 1978, matter-of-factly details the complaints of the bazaaris about the SAVAK:

BAZAARIS EXPRESSED GENERAL COMPLAINTS AGAINST THE SHAH SIMILAR TO THOSE HEARD ELSEWHERE, I.E., CORRUPTION OF HIGH-LEVEL OFFICIALS, MURDER AND TORTURE OF OPPOSITIONISTS, OVER-CONCENTRATION OF POWER AND POOR ECONOMIC DECISIONMAKING. HOWEVER, BAZAARIS CONCENTRATED THEIR IRE ON SAVAK AND ITS FORMER CHIEF NEMATOLLAH NASSIRI. SAVAK UNDER NASSIRI, THEY SAID, HAS KILLED AND TORUTURED (sic.) THOUSANDS OF PEOPLE. DURING THE IMPRISONMENT OF THE AYATOLLAH TALEGHANI, SAVAK

JAILORS HAD RAPED THE WOMEN IN HIM [His] HOME
AND FORCED TALEGHANI TO DRINK HIS JAILORS'
URINE.[25]

According to AI, when asked about torture in Iran, the Shah never
denied it, indeed quipping to a reporter of Le Monde on October 1,
1976, "Why should we not employ the same methods as you Europe-
ans? We have learned sophisticated methods of torture from you."[26]
Touché!

The SAVAK did not limit its ruthless work to the four corners of
Iran. Rather, as was well known at the time, and reported on by AI,
the SAVAK's tentacles reached into many nations of the world, including the United States, where the SAVAK was able to harass and hound
Iranian opposition figures and student radicals living abroad.

This even became an issue for the US Congress which carried out
some investigations into the SAVAK's operations in the United States.
For example, a cable on WikiLeaks describes an August 5, 1976, hear-
ing before the House Subcommittee on International Organizations
where a William Butler from the International Committee of Jurists
testified. The cable summarizes Mr. Butler as saying:

SAVAK HAS COMPLETE JURISDICTION OVER POLITICAL
CASES AND CRIMES AGAINST THE STATE OR THE SHAH.
IN ADDITION TO ITS ORGANIZATION OF SOME 200,000
FULL TIME OPERATIVES IN IRAN, SAVAK IS ALSO ACTIVE
IN OTHER COUNTRIES, NOTABLY THE U.S. AND FRG.[27]

In addition, the Shah's repression was not reserved only for Iranians.
Thus, the Shah, always the willing pawn of the West, helped oppress
others at the West's behest. For example, the Shah sent four thousand
troops, thirty helicopters, and Iranian naval vessels to aid the British
in their brutal, counterrevolutionary operation in Oman in the early
to mid-1970s.[28] In this instance, the Shah was aiding the British in

securing its oil and financial interests in the quite impoverished Oman nation against revolutionary forces who wanted an end to British colonial rule, and who had the temerity to demand "basic female emancipation" and "to limit men to having only one wife." This simply would not do, and the Shah was there to lend a hand to the British to prevent it.

It is impossible for me to think of Iran, or of the United States' long-time relationship with it, without thinking of the Shah's violent reign and the SAVAK, which carried out torture on a massive scale to keep the Shah in power. To me, the very existence of the SAVAK belies any claims that the United States somehow cares about human rights, democracy, or freedom, or that it wants such things for the Iranian people.

And certainly, the Iranian people must be forgiven if they do not believe that the United States has their best interests at heart. Indeed, knowing about the SAVAK, and the United States' critical role in creating and supporting it, leads me to feel no offense, and certainly no surprise, to hear that some Iranians to this day continue to chant "Death to America," or continue to label the United States "the Great Satan."

Iranians have every reason and right to feel anger and even hatred toward the United States, not just for what has been done to them, but also because the United States continues to do so while holding itself out as a bright beacon of democracy and freedom in the world. The US pretense of being a uniquely righteous country must be hard to bear for many in the world, not just the Iranians. And in truth, it has become unbearable for me, and I live here!

6

JIMMY CARTER AND THE HUMAN RIGHTS DOUBLE STANDARD

*We should cease to talk about vague and unreal objectives such
as human rights, the raising of living standards, and democratization.
The day is not far off when we are going to have to deal in straight
power concepts. The less we are then hampered by idealistic
slogans, the better.*
—George Kennan, 1948

A NEWLY-RELEASED STATE DEPARTMENT MEMO, DATED May 17, 2017, and entitled "Balancing Interests and Values," is a rare document in which the State Department openly and candidly articulates its long-held view that the United States must apply a double standard to human rights to advance US global interests.

This memo, from policy aide Brian Hook to Secretary of State Rex Tillerson, explicitly reminds Tillerson to make sure to treat allies and adversaries differently when it comes to expressing human rights concerns.[1] As Hook explains to Tillerson:

In the case of US allies such as Egypt, Saudi Arabia, and the Philippines, the Administration is fully justified in emphasizing good relations for a variety of important reasons, including counter-terrorism, and in honestly facing up to the difficult tradeoffs with regard to human rights. It is not as though human rights practices will be improved if anti-American radicals take power in those countries. Moreover, this would be a severe blow to our vital interests. We saw what a disaster Egypt's Muslim Brotherhood turned out to be in power. After eight years of Obama, the US is right to bolster US allies rather than badger or abandon them.

One useful guideline for a realistic and successful foreign policy is that allies should be treated differently—and better—than adversaries. Otherwise, we end up with more adversaries, and fewer allies. The classic dilemma of balancing ideals and interests is with regard to America's allies. In relation to our competitors, there is far less of a dilemma. We do not look to bolster America's adversaries overseas; we look to pressure, compete with, and outmaneuver them. For this reason, we should consider human rights as an important issue in regard to US relations with China, Russia, North Korea, and Iran. And this is not only because of moral concern for practices inside those countries. It is also because pressing those regimes on human rights is one way to impose costs, apply counter-pressure, and regain the initiative from them strategically.

Meanwhile, Hook criticizes the foreign policy of Jimmy Carter which he sees as an outlier amongst US presidents in the postwar era:

President Carter upended Cold War policies by criticizing and even undermining governments, especially in cases such as Nicaragua and Iran. The results were unfortunate for American interests, as for the citizens of those countries. Carter's badgering of American allies unintentionally strengthened anti-American radicals in both Iran and Nicaragua. As Jeanne Kirkpatrick wrote in 1979 criticizing Carter's foreign policy, "Hurried efforts to force complex and unfamiliar political practices on societies lacking the requisite political culture, tradition, and social structures not only fail to produce the desired outcomes; if they are undertaken at a time when the traditional regime is under attack, they actually facilitate the job of the insurgents."

Kirkpatrick's view of human rights is certainly the prevailing one amongst US policy-makers. This view was expressed very well in a March 6, 1975, legal advice memo to the State Department which can be found on WikiLeaks:

2500 YEARS AGO, PERSIAN EMPIRE SET NEW STANDARDS OF HUMAN RIGHTS FOR CONQUERED PEOPLES AND MINORITIES. TODAY IRAN'S CONSTITUTIONAL MONAR-CHY HARKS BACK TO GLORY AND POWER OF THAT ERA, BUT WORLD'S EXPECTATIONS IN HUMAN RIGHTS FIELD ARE HIGHER AND IRAN IS NO LONGER LEADER IN THAT FIELD. . . . IN ASSESSING PROTECTION OF HUMAN RIGHTS IN IRAN, WE MUST BE CAREFUL NOT TO PROJECT OUR OWN VALUES DIRECTLY ONTO THE IRANIAN SCENE.[2]

Meanwhile, now that Iran is considered an adversary of the United States, we are free to "project our values directly onto the Iranian scene" as much as we would like.

While I believe that Carter's human rights credentials are greatly overstated, the criticisms of Carter expressed by Jeanne Kirkpatrick, foreign policy adviser to Ronald Reagan during his 1980 campaign and then US ambassador to the UN, were shared by many in the US political and intelligence establishment. Therefore, Carter had to go, and by any means necessary. And, the means used were as nasty as one can imagine.

As the late, great Robert Parry, who exposed the "October Surprise," explains, "The right-wing complaint against Carter, as enunciated by Ronald Reagan and other conservatives, was that the President had let the Shah of Iran fall, had allowed the Sandinistas to claim power in Nicaragua and had undermined anti-communist regimes in South America and elsewhere by criticizing their human rights records as they used 'death squads' and torture to eliminate leftists" and others as well.[3] Meanwhile, the Israeli government "was livid with Carter over the Camp David Accords in which Israel had been pressured to return the Sinai to Egypt. [Prime Minister] Begin and his inner circle were alarmed at the prospect of a reelected Carter pressuring Israel to give up the West Bank too."

As Parry explains, in response to these alleged "crimes" of Carter, senior Republicans, including George H.W. Bush (former CIA director and then Reagan's running mate), high-level CIA officers not appointed by Carter, and Israeli intelligence used long-time assets in Tehran—assets which both the United States and Israel had cultivated for years under the Shah—to prevail upon the Iranian hostage takers to hold the American hostages at the former US Embassy longer in order to undermine Carter's chances at re-election. Parry writes, "The idea was that by persuading the Iranians to hold the 52 American hostages until after the U.S. presidential election, Carter would be made to look weak and inept, essentially dooming his hopes for a second term."

According to Parry, Israeli intelligence agent Ari Ben-Menashe, among other "October Surprise" witnesses, gave sworn testimony about the "meetings between Republicans and Iranians in 1980 that were designed with the help of CIA personnel and Israeli intelligence to delay release of the 52 hostages until after Carter's defeat."

Parry quite correctly compares this coup plot against Carter to the plot against Mossadegh, though, of course, the target of the coup plot in this case was a sitting US president. There is probably no better illustration of the United States' habitual overthrow of foreign governments coming back to haunt us, and our own democracy, than this event. And, it should not be surprising that the chickens would come back to roost in this way. When any individual or institution (e.g., the CIA) becomes too comfortable with making deals with devils to obtain such ends as regime change elsewhere, it is but one small step beyond this to making such deals to implement regime change at home. In this way, the CIA and its immoral coup plotting has become a grave danger to our own republic, or what is left of it.

Carter can aptly be compared to Mossadegh in at least one other respect—just as Mossadegh, Carter did not really pose a threat to US foreign policy objectives or practices. In the case of Carter, he never represented a real threat to the nearly invariable US practice of ignoring the human rights abuses of US allies. Simply put, Carter did not represent the sea change in US human rights and foreign policy that he is given credit, or blame, for depending upon which perspective one has of such matters.

As Fairness and Accuracy in Reporting (FAIR) relates, Carter continued to back such dictators as Ferdinand Marcos, and he increased military aid to Indonesia even as it was massacring hundreds of thousands of innocents in East Timor.[4]

Another good example of Carter's business-as-usual approach to foreign policy is El Salvador, a "death squad" state which Carter funded through some of its worst crimes. Indeed, Carter disregarded the personal plea made to him by a letter, dated February 19, 1980, from Archbishop Oscar Romero who, appealing to Carter's Christian faith and stated commitment to human rights, begged Carter to stop funding the Salvadoran military.

Archbishop Romero had been a quite conservative priest in El Salvador, and indeed was elevated to archbishop by Pope Paul VI precisely because he was seen as someone who would not rock the boat too much. Romero was transformed, however, when his friend, Father Rutilio Grande, was murdered, along with a teenager and an old man who happened to be with him, by Salvadoran police. Romero became radicalized by this experience and became an outspoken advocate for the poor and oppressed and against state repression.

A number of clerics were killed in the course of El Salvador's internal conflict. Indeed, when I was an international observer of El

Salvador's first elections after the civil war in 1994, I stayed on the floor of a church and slept under the photos of Father Grande and several other priests killed during this period.

In Romero's eloquent letter to Carter, which I reproduce in its entirety as it could have been written on behalf of so many peoples victimized by US aggression, he stated:

> In these last days there has appeared in the national press a report that troubles me deeply. According to it, your government is studying the possibility of supporting and aiding economically and militarily the government junta [of El Salvador].
>
> Because you are a Christian and because you manifested that you wish to defend human rights, I dare to expose my pastoral point of view regarding this news and make a concrete petition to you.
>
> I am deeply troubled by the news that the government of the United States should be studying the way to favor the militarist path of El Salvador by sending military equipment and advisors to "train three Salvadoran battalions in logistics, communications and intelligence." In the event that this journalistic information is true, your government's contribution, rather than favoring greater justice and peace in El Salvador will make injustice and repression against the organization of the people, who have been struggling for the respect of their most fundamental rights, even more acute.
>
> The current ruling Junta, and above all the armed forces and security forces, have unfortunately not demonstrated their capacity to resolve the grave national problems through political practice and structural means. In general, they have only resorted to repressive violence, producing a volume of dead and wounded that is greater than that of recent military regimes whose systematic violation of human rights was condemned by the Inter-American Commission on Human Rights.
>
> The brutal way in which the security forces recently evicted and assassinated the occupants of the headquarters of the Christian

Democratic Party despite that the Junta and the government (it would appear) did not authorize that operation is evidence that the Junta and the Christian Democrats do not govern the country, but rather, the political power is in the hands of military men without scruples, who only know how to oppress the people and favor the interests of the Salvadoran oligarchy.

If it is true that this past November, "a group of six Americans spent time in El Salvador supplying two hundred thousand dollars' worth of gas masks and bullet proof vests and instructing on their use against demonstrators," you yourself must know that clearly since then the security forces, acting with greater personal protection and effectiveness, have repressed the people even more violently, using deadly weapons.

As such, given the fact that as a Salvadoran, and as Archbishop of the Archdiocese of San Salvador, I have the obligation to watch so that faith and justice reign in my country, I ask that if you truly want to defend human rights:

– You prohibit this military aid to the Salvadoran government.

– You guarantee that your government not intervene directly or indirectly with military, economic and diplomatic pressure.

At this time, we are living through a grave economic and political crisis in our country, but it is doubtless that each time the people have increased their conscience and their organization and have empowered themselves to become the driving force which is responsible for the future of El Salvador, and the only one capable of overcoming this crisis.

It would be unjust and deplorable that by the interference of foreign powers the Salvadoran people were frustrated, they were repressed, and impeded in deciding with autonomy over the economic and political trajectory that our country should follow.

It would suppose violating a right that the Latin American bishops gathered in Puebla publicly acknowledged when we said: "The legitimate self-determination of our countries that permits them to

organize according to their own disposition and history, and to cooperate in a new international order..." (Puebla Synod, 505.)

I hope that your religious convictions and your sensibilities in
pro defense of human rights will compel you to accept my petition,
avoiding with it a major spilling of blood in my long-suffered
country.[5]

Sadly for Romero, he just did not understand the fact that US foreign
policy is not guided by such fanciful things as Christianity, human
rights, morality, or just plain human decency. Rather, it is guided by
the will to power and wealth, even despite the lofty rhetoric of such
leaders as President Carter.

And so, Carter did not even have the decency to reply to Romero
himself, but instead gave the honor of a reply to Secretary of State
Cyrus Vance who sent a patronizing note back, making it clear that the
United States would continue to double down on the Salvadoran military. As Vance wrote on March 1, 1980:

> The President has asked that I respond to your letter of February 17
> regarding the situation in El Salvador and expressing your frank
> views on United States assistance to the Revolutionary Junta of Gov-
> ernment. We are pleased to see confirmed that you and the President
> have many goals and concerns in common. As you note, the advance-
> ment of human rights has been and remains one of the principal
> foreign policy goals of our government and I assure you that it under-
> lies every aspect of United States policy towards El Salvador.
>
> The Revolutionary Junta of Government has shown itself to be
> moderate and reformist. The United States, dedicated by tradition
> and long practice to democratic principles, is anxious about El Salva-
> dor's grave political crisis and stands ready to contribute to peaceful
> and progressive solutions. We believe the reform program of the Rev-
> olutionary Junta of Government offers the best prospect for peaceful

change toward a more just society. We therefore have responded to the Junta's request for our assistance to help carry out its goals. . . .

We appreciate your warnings about the dangers of providing military assistance given the traditional role of the security forces in El Salvador. As we consider any request for such assistance, I can assure you that whatever military assistance may be provided will be directed at helping the government to break with this tradition and to defend and carry forward its announced program of reform and development. We are as concerned as you that any assistance we provide not be used in a repressive manner. Therefore, any equipment and training which we might provide would be designed to overcome the most serious deficiencies of the armed forces, enhancing their professionalism so that they can fulfill their essential role of maintaining order with a minimum of lethal force.

I believe there is no real contradiction between proper law enforcement and respect for human rights. I will use our influence to avert any misuse of our assistance in ways that injure human rights of the people of El Salvador and will promptly reassess our assistance should evidence of such misuse develop. However, we hope you will agree that a less confrontational environment is necessary to implement the kind of meaningful reform program you have long advocated.

I thank you for sharing your concerns with us and assure you that your views are being given careful consideration by the President and the United States Government. I believe that we are all committed to the advancement of human rights and democratic principles. We share a repugnance for the violence provoked by both extremes that is taking the lives of innocent people. We deplore the efforts of those seeking to silence the voices of reason and moderation with explosives, intimidation, and murder, the great, moral authority of the Church, and your uncompromising defense of human rights and dedication to non-violence convince me that our shared values can be the basis of a cooperative effort in search of peaceful solutions.

The United States will not interfere in the internal affairs of El Salvador. Nevertheless, we are gravely concerned that the threat of civil war in your country could endanger the security and well-being of the whole Central American region. We shall continue to do what we can to respond to the legitimate requests of the Revolutionary Junta of Government in its efforts to correct economic and social injustice and promote respect for democratic procedures and the rights of the individual.

I wish you every success in carrying out your heavy pastoral responsibilities amid the new demands that the threat of civil war has imposed on you. You have a major role to play in helping your fellow countrymen find peaceful solutions to their problems. May God give you wisdom and strength in this difficult task.[6]

Despite Cyrus Vance's well-wishes, Archbishop Romero would be unable to carry out his "heavy pastoral responsibilities" much longer, for within a mere three weeks of receiving this letter, he himself was killed by the security forces of the "moderate and reformist" Salvador government which he had warned Carter about. He was killed just after saying mass. And, in his last sermon before his death, as recounted by Noam Chomsky and Edward S. Herman in their landmark book, *Manufacturing Consent*, Romero "appealed to members of the army and the security forces to refuse to kill their Salvadoran brethren, a call that enraged the officer corps trying to build a lower-class military that was willing to kill freely."[7]

Even Romero's assassination, or Christian martyrdom as many around the world believe it to be, did not move Carter into halting military aid to El Salvador. Indeed, quite to the contrary, as Chomsky and Herman explain, "The Carter Administration had been so disturbed by Romero's opposition to its policies that it had secretly lobbied the pope to curb the archbishop."

Carter was given a bit of pause, however, when, in December of the same year (1980), four American church women of the Catholic Maryknoll religious order were brutally raped and murdered by right-wing death squad forces closely aligned with the Salvadoran military. Carter did suspend military aid to El Salvador just after this event, but then quickly reinstated it within weeks, and just in time to turn over the reins to Ronald Reagan who would really ramp up the repression in El Salvador.

In short, Carter never lived up to all the hype of his self-proclaimed human rights presidency. And, when it came to his policy with regard to Iran and the Shah, Carter would act just as all the presidents before him, backing the Shah even as he killed thousands of civilians in a last-ditch effort to cling to power.

Meanwhile, lest the events in El Salvador in the 1980s seem too remote from the subject of this book, it is important to note that the United States has consciously utilized the "Salvador option" in countries like Iraq and Afghanistan to put down insurgencies, and the United States even called upon veterans of the war in El Salvador to help.

Thus, as the *Guardian* of London explained, Retired Colonel Jim Steele, who headed up special forces advisers in El Salvador in the 1980s, was recruited to serve as "secretary Donald Rumsfeld's personal envoy to Iraq's Special Police Commandos. . . ."[8] The *Guardian*, which could easily have been describing El Salvador's death squad units, characterized the Iraqi Special Police Commandos as "a fearsome paramilitary force that ran a secret network of detention centres across the country—where those suspected of rebelling against the US-led invasion were tortured for information."

As the *Guardian* related, the job of advising and training brutal paramilitary force in Iraq "was a role made for Steele. The veteran had made his name in El Salvador almost 20 years earlier as head of a US group of special forces advisers who were training and funding the Salvadoran military to fight the FMLN guerrilla insurgency. These government units developed a fearsome international reputation for their death squad activities."

The *Guardian* further notes, in an unintentional rebuke to Cyrus Vance who claimed to Archbishop Romero that the Carter Administration was seeking "peaceful and progressive solutions" in El Salvador, that "the arming of one side of the conflict by the US [which began under Carter] hastened the country's descent into a civil war in which 75,000 people died and 1 million out of a population of 6 million became refugees." And, while Vance in his letter decried the violence on both sides of the political spectrum in El Salvador, it was in truth the forces which the United States funded which carried out the lion's share of the violence. Thus, as El Salvador's Truth Commission would later conclude, "85% of 'serious acts of violence' were attributed to the state" which the United States backed throughout the conflict.

In truth, the United States' "Salvador option," or option of creating, training, and arming indigenous paramilitary death squad units to destroy local insurgencies, really began in Colombia in the early 1960s, was then carried out in Vietnam, and continues to this day in countries such as Afghanistan and Syria.

And so, Romero's words to Carter shortly before his death ring as powerful and true as they did then, and they continue to be ignored by successive US presidents.

7

THE SHAH'S REIGN BEGINS TO CRUMBLE

IF YOU WATCH THE MOVIE *ARGO*, you will see the quite amusing scene of young people in the former US Embassy pasting together the confidential and secret documents which the Embassy staff had feverishly shredded before the hostage-taking in 1980. This amazing puzzle-like project did take place, and, over many years, the documents were put back together.

As journalist Robert Fisk explains:

A team of twenty students was gathered to work on the papers. A flat board was fitted with elastic bands to hold the shreds in place. They could reconstruct five to ten documents a week. They were the carpet-weavers, carefully, almost lovingly re-threading their tapestry. Iranian carpets are filled with flowers and birds, the recreation of a garden in the desert; they were intended to give life amid sand and heat, to create eternal meadows amid a wasteland. The Iranians who worked for months on those shredded papers were creating their own unique carpet, one that exposed the past and was transformed into a living history book amid the arid propaganda of the revolution. High-school students and disabled war veterans were enlisted to work on this carpet of papers. It would take them six years to complete, 3,000 pages containing 2,300 documents, all eventually contained in 85 volumes.[1]

The documents painstakingly put back together by the Iranians, known as the "Documents from the U.S. Espionage Den," are now online and make for fascinating reading.[2] They detail the final years of the Shah and the support the United States would give him until the very end. Unless otherwise noted, I cite those documents here in a short history of the fall of the last Shah of Iran.

The last few years of the Shah were marked by huge protests and equally massive repression in response. As a December 5, 1978, State Department cable I discovered on WikiLeaks related:

DOMONSTRATIONS (sic.): ACCORDING TO JAFFARI, NIGHT OF DEC 2 WAS PARTICULARLY VIOLENT IN BAZAAR AREA. TROOPS KILLED SOME 300 DEMONSTRATORS. JAFFARI CLAIMED TO HAVE SEEN THE SHOOTING AND THE BODIES LITTERING SAR CHESHMEH STREET. DURING CLEANUP THE SHOES LEFT LYING IN THE STREET FILLED TWO LARGE GUNNY[3]

Robert Fisk describes a demonstration with much greater numbers of casualties. As he explains, "Street marches in Tehran were more than a million strong. Revolutionary literature still claims that the Shah's army killed 4,000 demonstrators in Jaleh Square in Tehran on 8 September," 1978.[4]

Imagine: Four thousand people killed in one demonstration! If such a thing happened in Venezuela or Cuba, or in Iran in 2018, this would be cause for the United States to send in the 82nd Airborne. In addition, such an event would be cause for great media fanfare if it happened, say, in China, for example, during the Tiananmen Square protests ten years later in which three hundred to three thousand protestors were killed.

The Tiananmen Square protests and massacre live in infamy, and in the collective consciousness, while the Jaleh Square massacre in Tehran is forgotten in the West, if it was ever known about to begin with. But again, the Jaleh Square massacre happened in the Shah's Iran, and the West happily supported this repression. The "Documents from the U.S. Espionage Den" prove this.

For example, a telegram from the US Embassy in Tehran (Secret), dated November 2, 1978, discusses the following topic: "Looking Ahead: The Military Option." Here, the Embassy talks about the Shah's stated option of a military takeover as a last-ditch effort to protect his reign. As the Embassy explains:

> Any takeover would have to involve a very hard crack-down on demonstrators in the streets, students and professors demonstrating in the universities, school children and teachers demonstrating in the schools, religious leaders and their bazaari merchant backers, left-wingers and all sorts, and sufficient numbers of striking workers to get all strikers back on the job. Some curbs on the press would be inevitable. The momentum of this operation would involve thousands of arrests, among the first probably being many of the political prisoners that have been released over the past year or two. . . . Given the pro-government passivity of large areas of the countryside (many of them inhabited by Sunni Moslem tribes who were pacified by Reza Shah and the present Shah not long ago) the army should be able to handle disturbances outside the larger cities. For urban purposes, the police and SAVAK would have to be given a freer hand than in recent months, perhaps assisted by some of military intelligence in whom the army high command would have greater confidence. To be effective the takeover would have to turn Iran back in to the tightly controlled state it was before liberalization began in mid-1976.
>
> We are quiet [sic.] sure this can be done—but at a cost.[5]

The Embassy, referring to the United States' crimes in other theaters of the world, sets forth some of the possible costs: "The international outcry in the U.S and elsewhere would reach new decibel levels. The situation would in this sense be less comparable to Lebanon today than to the regime of the Colonels in Greece or to Latin American Juntas over the years. Blood-shed would increase and affect larger numbers of the population than ever before in Pahlavi history."[6]

However, the Embassy of Jimmy "Human Rights" Carter made it clear that this was a price which may have to be paid to allow our partner in crime, the Shah, to cling to power: "Our long association with the Shah's regime and his army would make us a target for the accusation that we were behind the takeover and continuing to support it against the will of the Iranian people. *Perhaps this will prove to be an unavoidable penalty we will have to pay*, but we should be under no illusion that a penalty it will be, counting against us in world public opinion and probably returning to haunt us in Iran once the military regime has run its course."[7]

This document is signed by William Sullivan, Carter's ambassador to Iran.

At this point, it may be of value to revisit the United States involvement in the rise of the "Colonels in Greece" and the Juntas in Latin America. Just after WWII, Britain and the United States intervened in the Greek civil war on behalf of the fascists against the Greek left which had successfully ousted the Nazis from Greece—a formidable feat given that Britain had intervened during WWII against the left-wing guerillas. With the help of Britain and the United States, the fascists prevailed in the post-WWII civil war in Greece and "instituted a highly brutal regime, for which the CIA created a suitably repressive internal security agency (KYP in Greek),"[8] just as it had helped create the repressive SAVAK in Iran. The fascist government erected a statue of Harry S. Truman in Athens as thanks for the United States' role in the coup under his leadership. This statue has been blown up, rebuilt, and blown up again several times.

And then, much to the chagrin of both Britain and America, democracy broke out again in Greece—the country which, as we all know, invented democracy—when liberal George Papandreou was elected in 1964. Just before the 1967 elections which Papandreou was sure to win again, a joint effort of Britain, the CIA, Greek Military, KYP and US military stationed in Greece brought about a military coup which brought the fascists back to power. And, as with the Shah in Iran, the new rightist government immediately instituted "martial law, censorship, arrests, beatings, and killing, the victims totaling 8,000 in the first month. . . . Torture, inflicted in the most gruesome ways, often with equipment supplied by the United States, became routine."[9] Sound familiar?

As for the Latin American Juntas brought to power and/or backed by the United States, these are too numerous to detail in a book on Iran, but a short list would include the following: the genocidal military dictatorship brought to power in 1954 (just after the Iranian coup) in Guatemala, again by the Dulles brothers who successfully overthrew the democratic presidency of Jacobo Arbenz in the interests of the United Fruit Company in which both brothers had an interest; the rightist and repressive military government brought to power in 1964 in Brazil through a CIA-backed coup to destroy the burgeoning Liberation Theology Movement there; the Pinochet dictatorship in Chile which the CIA helped bring to power in the interest of such companies as ITT and Kennecott Copper, overthrowing democratically-elected President Salvador Allende in the process; the fascist Argentine Junta which the United States helped come to power and then supported as it famously disappeared thirty thousand dissidents, many times stealing their children in the process and giving them over to loyal, rightist families; the murderous military dictatorship in El Salvador which the Carter and Reagan Administrations backed to the hilt as it was responsible for killing about 80 percent of the seventy-five thousand civilians murdered during its reign.

In short, the story is not a pretty one, and William Sullivan, who, during the US war on Vietnam personally oversaw the massive and

secret bombing of Laos[10]—Laos suffering the greatest bombing bar-
rage ever in human history—was quite aware how the world viewed the
United States in light of its role in helping bring about and defend
some of the most brutal regimes in the world.

And yet, when considering what he believed to be the possible
necessity of the Shah—only one in a line of so many repressive dictators sponsored by the United States—to defend his regime with further
brutality, Sullivan opined that such brutality, and the global outrage
that would surely follow against the United States, was probably worth
it. And, Sullivan was the ambassador to Iran, as he had been the
ambassador to Laos. So much for diplomacy!

As the United States today is estimated to provide military support
to about 73 percent of the world's dictatorships,[11] one must wonder at
what point the many exceptions to the United States as defender of
democracy and freedom in the world have swallowed the rule, and
whether the United States has any moral authority at all to decide
which governments, or "regimes," will stay or go. I would argue stren-
uously that even assuming, *arguendo*, that any nation has such authority,
whether legal, moral, or otherwise—a quite dubious proposition to
begin with—the United States lost such moral authority long ago.

Another telegram from Ambassador Sullivan dated November 8,
1978, shows the depth of the Iranians' anger towards the Shah for his
crimes against them. Talking about some of the demonstrations in
Iran, Sullivan writes:

> Bazaaris led off with passionate rehearsal of Shah's sins over past 5-6
> years and that of people who have surrounded him such as SAVAK's
> Nassiri. Almost every family has someone who has been killed or
> gone to prison.
>
> They detailed specific cases of political prisoners such as one
> Farhad Menukade and his brother who were arrested for possession
> of religious books by Ayatollah Khomeini and have been in Qasr
> Prison for four years. . . . There are other examples of some 3 to 4

thousand political prisoners they believe are still being held in jail. Only better known cases have been released. Visitors to these prisons are badly treated by officials. . . . The Govt has burned mosques. They have imposed controls on the bazaar—breaking the network which assured them due representation in the govt.[12]

An airgram from the American Consul in Shiraz to the Department of State, dated November 21, 1978, shows that US diplomats were quite aware of why the people of Iran were rising up against their man in Tehran:

The intractability of anti-regime sentiment relates to its extent and the profundity with which it is felt among members of the Iranian population at large. Opposition has assumed a highly moral basis, whether it be in terms of reaction to the secularization of the state and the gross materialism of the *nouveau riche* or the perception that the Shah, his family and his coterie represent evil incarnate. . . . Corruption, too, must be viewed in these terms. Its degree of pervasiveness is less important than its symbolic value in the popular mind for the inherent evil of the Pahlavi dynasty. This issue, along with degeneracy in high places and institutionalized torture, has taken on a political reality of its own in recent weeks.[13]

However, the fact that the Shah represented "evil incarnate" to the Iranians, was not cause for the US to abandon him. Thus, just two days later, on November 30, 1978, Ambassador Sullivan sent a telegram to the secretary of state saying that, "while we realize distrust which most opposition leaders have in Shah's promises, we believe it is unrealistic to insist on Shah's abdication."[14]

And, Jimmy Carter himself found a way to communicate with the Shah his continued support of him, even in the eleventh hour of his rule. Thus, in a letter dated December 1, 1978, W. W. Blumenthal, the secretary of the treasury, addresses his "Imperial Majesty" (the Shah), and told him: "I have reported to President Carter on our conversation and he has asked me to repeat to you his firm intention to support your efforts to restore civil order and to move toward a broadly-based civilian government as soon as circumstances permit."[15] Carter's message to the Shah, in other words, was: keep up the military rule and the bloodletting until the people are sufficiently beaten down, and then get back to "civilian" rule—meaning continued rule by the Shah and his SAVAK—when you feel like it.

In this same letter, we learn why Carter is continuing to back the Shah and his imposition of martial law—Oil! Thus, Blumenthal tells the Shah, "I particularly appreciate the role you expect Iran to play at the forthcoming OPEC Conference. Moderation in setting petroleum prices will be vitally important for the success of the President's efforts to combat inflation and to correct the unwarranted decline of the dollar."[16]

Here, we see that Carter was really not so much different than any other president, in the end caring more about profane things like oil than such lofty issues as human rights. And indeed, in his State of the Union Address, on January 23, 1980, Carter would announce the plan which would govern US policy in the Middle East to this day. Now known as "the Carter Doctrine," this policy provides that the United States will use military force if necessary to defend its interests (again, meaning oil) in the Persian Gulf. An extension of the Monroe Doctrine, and its Roosevelt Corollary, which provide that the United States may intervene in its "backyard" of Latin America and the Caribbean at any time to defend its interests, Carter was now announcing that the reach of the United States extended throughout the world.

A number of these documents, like nearly all public pronouncements of the US foreign policy establishment, show a feigned surprise at how the United States, and Israel as well, are viewed in all of this. Thus, in a telegram to the US Embassy in London, and dated December 2, 1978, the US secretary of state says, with no apparent irony: "The USG is frequently accused by the opposition as having installed the Shah and keeping him in power. Israel is sometimes depicted as a junior partner of the U.S."[17]

The US government is accused of installing and supporting the Shah? This is presented as a mere accusation just one day after President Carter had pledged allegiance to the Shah even as his regime was in its death throes. And Israel, whose Mossad had also been training the SAVAK, is a junior partner of the United States? This reminds me of the line in the movie *Casablanca*, when Captain Louis Renault exclaims, "I am shocked—shocked—to find that gambling is going on in here!" This is meant to be a funny line, because he obviously knows that gambling is going on in the saloon. The similar line of the secretary of state would be funny too, if it weren't so downright infuriating.

In this same telegram, the secretary of state shows that he knows the end may be near for the Shah. Thus, he discusses what a possible new government might look like if the Shah is overthrown, stating that it "would probably project militant nationalism, Islam and (probably) socialism, with intentions of non-alignment, non-interventionism, and anti-Western rhetoric. Ties with Israel and South Africa would be cut." He was mostly right with his predictions, showing that he knew more than his other statement might let on. The only part that would not really come to fruition was the "socialism" part; that was seen to by the Shah's brutal suppression of the Iranian left with the strong support of the United States.

As for the breaking of ties with both Israel and South Africa, that did happen right after the 1979 Revolution, with the new government arguing that it would not have relations with either country which it viewed to be apartheid states. In breaking ties with Apartheid South Africa, Iran would indeed show an enlightenment that neither the United States nor Israel had, with the two latter countries supporting Apartheid South Africa almost to the bitter end. For its part, the United States, whose CIA helped arrest Nelson Mandela back in 1962, leading to his twenty-seven-year incarceration, would keep Mr. Mandela on its "terrorist list" until 2008. In the case of Israel, the only nuclear state in the Middle East with about two hundred nuclear missiles, it received much of its uranium for its nuclear program from the Apartheid South African government.

Another revealing little document is a letter from the office of the director of Central Intelligence. This letter, specifically from the CIA's Deputy Director for National Foreign Assessment Robert R. Bowie to Bill (Ambassador William Sullivan), is dated December 14, 1978, and reads, in pertinent part, "My special thanks for your hosting the cocktail party, which enabled me to have some less formal conversations with several Iranian military and SAVAK people."[18] Incredibly, the United States has done its level best to claim that it was not tied to the SAVAK, but here you have a high-ranking CIA official meeting with "SAVAK people" about a month and a half before the Shah would be driven out of power. Even more revealing, it appears that the US ambassador hosted these "SAVAK people" at an Embassy cocktail party.

The hits keep coming, with the US diplomatic staff acknowledging another big issue the people had with the Shah beyond his systematic torture of them, and that was rampant corruption which many times took the form of misuse and misappropriation of US financial and economic assistance—assistance the United States refused to give to poor Mohammad Mossadegh. Thus, in a Dec. 15, 1978, air gram from the American Consul in Shiraz (yes, that is where the famous wine originally came from) to the Department of State, the author writes,

Corruption has become a major political issue in Iran in recent weeks, with much criticism of the Shah being couched in terms of the corrupt activities of some of his closest advisors and even members of his family. The outrage which has emerged against the phenomenon is certainly widespread, cutting across social and economic class lines, and it appears to be deeply felt. Further, corruption, as the term is usually defined, has unquestionably been a pervasive fact of Iranian life, and the magnitude of some of the rip-offs which have been in the news of late is impressive by any standard. It was perhaps inevitable that the vast amounts of money involved in many of the grandiose projects undertaken in Iran during the last decade would constitute temptations for illicit gains that could not be resisted.[19]

The corruption and greed of the Shah was indeed impressive. Today, one can visit his incredible golden palace in Tehran, now a museum, which is truly a site to behold. This is compared to the Ayatollahs, who, say what you will about them, have lived in very modest accommodations.

There is another telling line in the air gram from the Consul in Shiraz which is breathtaking in its matter-of-factness. Thus, the Consul states, "Even a man such as former Prime Minister Ali Amini appears more intent on blood than social equity in the distribution of economic wealth. He recently suggested that in view of the thousands of children who had been killed for reading proscribed literature (sic), it was not too much to ask that a hundred plutocrats be hanged."

Thousands of children killed for reading banned literature? Naturally one does a double take at this. But it was true. As the US diplomats in Iran were quite aware, children were killed in Iran for "crimes against the state." In his book, *Shah of Shahs*, Kapuscinski talks about a three-year-old prisoner of the SAVAK who was, as was very common, locked up with his whole family.

But this is what the United States was buying into in supporting the Shah, and support him the United States would. Thus, in a Department of State memo classified as "Secret/Nodis," and dated December 19, 1978, Henry Precht, who held the key position of Iran country director in the US State Department, candidly states what few would admit publicly, or even privately: "It will be extremely difficult for the U.S., which has supported one man for three decades and daily reaffirmed that support in the strongest terms during the past three months, to claim victory when he is dumped." Further in the memo, he reiterates that the US position in the Middle East "has been seriously weakened during the past three months because of our delayed perceptions, hesitancy to make hard choices, our unwavering support for the Shah and the anti-Americanism that has flourished."[20]

Precht's advice to the State Department is that "we should begin now to educate the Saudis and others about what the Shah's problem is, e.g., a loss of support and credibility because of corruption, harsh police methods, lack of political freedom, etc."

This a particularly revealing document, as it admits that the Carter Administration, despite its professed dedication to human rights, reaffirmed daily its support for the Shah even as it was becoming apparent that his days were numbered due to his own brutality and corruption, both of which the Carter Administration was quite aware of.

Moreover, as reflected in a "State Department Confidential Country Team Report of December 27, 1978," the Carter Administration was quite aware that Khomeini was publicly pleading with him "to pull back from his strong stands in support of the Shah."[21] This is reminiscent of Archbishop Romero's letter to Carter sometime later. And, as with the plea from Archbishop Romero, Carter would disregard Khomeini's plea as well.

Meanwhile, there is an interesting tidbit in the Country Team Report which reads, "The Ambassador opened the meeting by reviewing the rather disturbing . . . report that a young university Professor was killed by a shotgun wound. Troops have blocked off Eisenhower Ave. onto Shahreza Ave. . . . The Professor was shot from a long distance by a sniper while he spoke to crowds of students from a balcony. The Ambassador feels this shooting will touch off a large confrontation between demonstrators and security forces." Here was a description of a daily horror in Iran where it was open season on professors and intellectuals. Note also that, under the Shah, there was an Eisenhower Avenue, named of course after the US president that put the Shah in power. Do I need to mention that this street has since been renamed?

Other horrors are detailed throughout these documents from the US Embassy, or the Den of US Espionage, as the Iranians call it. One confidential letter, for example, from the secretary of state to the Embassy in Tehran, dated January 1979 (that is, about a month before the Shah would be toppled), notes that "possibly several thousand persons were killed in protests, several times that number injured," as a result of the fact that "these demonstrations were met by armed force as the security organs of the government sought to ban public protest activity."[22] The same letter notes that up to seven thousand people had been killed in clashes between the opposition and the government in the past year—a quite staggering figure by any standard.

In reflecting on this history, one must ask themselves if the United States, and specifically Jimmy Carter, had eased the Shah out earlier, could they have prevented the huge loss of life that occurred as the Shah violently tried to cling to power. And, maybe if the United States had done this, had heeded Khomeini's long-time plea to stop propping up the Shah—a plea dating back to the Kennedy Administration—the nature of the government that followed the Shah might also be different; possibly more friendly to the United States, possibly more open. We will never know, of course. But one would like to think that there are some lessons to learn here.

Similarly, had Carter not provided refuge to the Shah in October of 1979, there would never have been the hostage-taking at the US Embassy. Indeed, by all accounts, it was Carter's invitation to the Shah to obtain medical treatment for his cancer in New York that precipitated the hostage taking, which took place nine days after the Shah entered the United States.[23]

As Steven Kinzer relates, the students who took the Embassy staff hostage were painfully aware of the fact that the last time the Shah had gone into exile, he returned as the US-imposed monarch. The students—who, by the way, quickly released the women and African Americans among the group, with one of the African Americans, a Marine Guard, opining that the Revolution had been a good thing[24]—were not only enraged at Carter's invitation, but also desperately wanted to prevent a repeat of what happened in 1953. Their explicit demand for releasing the hostages was a return of the Shah to Iran to stand trial. That is, there was some method to the apparent madness of the hostage-takers.

In any case, just as Eisenhower had decided years before, Carter decided not to take the road less traveled; not to try to win favor with Iran, the Middle East, and the world by dumping the Shah of Iran. And many have paid a hefty price ever since as a consequence.

Meanwhile, to add insult to injury, President Carter refused to apologize for the United States' despicable role in installing and supporting the Shah. But of course, being an American president means never having to say you're sorry. As V.G. Kiernan, in his book on US imperialism, puts it so well:

Representing the apogee of human rights and humanitarian sentiments among post-war U.S. presidents, Carter also rebuffed Iranian demands for an apology from the U.S. for installing the Shah in power since 1953 and the subsequent decades of the S.A.V.A.K. torture that continued well into this 'soft' Democrat's administration: 'I don't think we have anything to apologize for,' assured Henry Kissinger. Ruminating about the United States of Amnesia, Carter's principal White House aide for Iran throughout the crisis, Mr. Gary Sick, admitted that from the standpoint of U.S. policy-makers 'anything that happened more than a quarter century before—even an event of singular importance—assumes the pale and distant appearance of ancient history. In Washington, by 1978, the events of 1953 had all the relevance of a pressed flower.' Barely over a year before the Iranian people toppled this modernizing despot, Carter toasted the Shah's Iran as 'an island of stability,' which he called a 'great tribute to the respect, admiration and love of your people for you'. A defiant George H.W. Bush announced, after the U.S. shot down a large Iranian airliner filled with 290 civilians, 'I will never apologize for the United States of America. I don't care what the facts are.' [25]

Of course, to the Iranians, with a history spanning thousands of years, the events of 1953 were like yesterday, and the support the United States gave to the Shah and the SAVAK up until the bitter end in 1979 were even fresher wounds. This calls to mind the story about Chinese premier Zhou Enlai being asked by Richard Nixon in 1972 about the significance of the 1789 French Revolution, whereupon Enlai, also from a country with an ancient history, quipped, "too early to say."

In truth, the well-documented amnesia that Americans have about historic events is selective, with Americans usually able to remember the tragedies they have suffered and the crimes committed against them, like the attacks of September 11, 2001, or the bombing of Pearl Harbor in 1941. Of course, in all fairness, Americans are kept in the dark about the less savory episodes in our collective history by both our schools and our press. At the same time, it seems to me that in addition to a lack of knowledge is a lack of empathy for others' suffering, as well as the complete refusal to accept the truth about the suffering our nation has inflicted on others even when we are told about it.

8

US FOREIGN POLICY AND THE RISE OF THE AYATOLLAH

WHEN THE IRANIAN REVOLUTION CAME, THE American people were ill-prepared by their government and press who, up to that point, had portrayed the Shah's reign as solid. Therefore, for the American people, the Revolution seemed to burst on the scene out of thin air, and the anti-US anger of the Iranian people, who burned US flags and effigies of Uncle Sam in the streets, seemed irrational and incomprehensible.

The intellectual and revolutionary Eqbal Ahmed, in an article written for *Mother Jones* right after the revolution,[1] describes how the US citizenry had been led to believe that the Shah was a great modernizer with, in the words of the *New York Times* in the summer of 1978, "a broad base of popular support." They had no idea, as Ahmed explains, of the more than twenty-five previous years of repression inflicted upon the Iranian people by the Shah, or that his brutality increased in proportion to the increase in US military aid. They had no idea that ten thousand demonstrators were killed in the last year of the Shah's reign, or of the anti-riot equipment sent by the United States to aid in the repression of demonstrators, or that Amnesty International had "described the Shah's regime as the world's worst human rights violator."

And, as Ahmed explains, the American people were kept in the dark about the realities of Iran by a Western press which was, and continues to be, deeply compromised by its obsequiousness to power. Thus, he relates the incredible story of William Safire, a *New York Times* columnist at the time of the 1979 Revolution. Safire, while a staffer for Richard Nixon in 1972, was shown what he noted as the "graciousness" of the Shah who, responding to Safire's whim to shop in the middle of the night, had the bazaaris rudely awakened from their slumber to accommodate him. Not surprisingly, given such treatment by the Shah, the bazaaris would become the backbone of the 1979 Islamic Revolution. And, not surprisingly, given Safire's flattery by the Shah—the type of flattery the Shah would show all his Western guests—Safire could not keep his readers up on the truth about his brutal reign.

In addition to being kept in the dark about the true nature of the Shah, Americans also had no idea about the man who would come to lead Iran after the Shah was deposed.

As Ahmed explains,

> The Western press has not known what to make of Ayatollah Ruhol-lah Khomeini. This 78-year-old man seems to have appeared out of nowhere with, unaccountably, millions of devoted followers in Iran. But Khomeini did indeed come from somewhere—the same national-ist coalition that periodically has emerged as resistance to foreign domination of Iran. He was a leader the last time his coalition pro-tested *en masse* in 1963, when large demonstrations protested the granting of immunity from Iranian law to U.S. military personnel.[2]

There is much ink spilled in the internal US documents preserved in the "Documents from the U.S. Espionage Den" about the controversial nature of this immunity bill, which the United States rammed through the Majlis and about the opposition of many Iranians, including

Khomeini himself, thereto. As these same documents describe, Khomeini would be exiled after the 1963 demonstrations, having been blamed by the Shah for the Shah's murder of children demonstrators who had been organized by Khomeini and his supporters. This was the classic case of the abuser blaming the victim for the former's own offenses. By the way, at the present time, the United States has bilateral immunity agreements with over one hundred countries, preventing its military personnel from being tried under the laws of these foreign countries for any crimes, including rape and murder.

Khomeini also came from the one place where people could escape the otherwise omnipresent tyranny of the Shah to try to organize and plan their futures—the mosques. In the words of Ahmed, "Politics in Iran was forced to take the cover of religion" by a totalitarian state enthusiastically installed and supported by the United States.

John F. Kennedy famously said, "Those who make peaceful revolution impossible will make violent revolution inevitable." This is, of course, true. Quite tragically, Kennedy, who initiated the National Security Doctrine to violently prevent social change in Latin America and who led the United States' deeper involvement into the effort to destroy Vietnam's bid for independence, never heeded his own words.

It is equally true, especially when talking about the Middle East, that those who make a secular, progressive revolution impossible will make a radical religious revolution inevitable. The United States and its partner Great Britain have made secular revolutions in the Middle East, and Iran in particular, impossible for many decades.

As just one example, Great Britain had supported the Muslim Brotherhood in Egypt as far back as 1928, as it identified it as "an anti-nationalist and anti-liberal vehicle" to be used against the pro-democracy forces in that country. It continued to back the Brotherhood against the government of Gamal Abdel Nasser, a secularist who had the audacity "to abolish the monarchy and establish a republic."[3] And indeed, just around the same time it was trying to overthrow Mossadegh in Iran, Britain was trying to assassinate Nasser, who represented the distinct danger of spreading secular democracy throughout the Arab world.[4]

As for Iran, when its revolution came in 1979, it was led by the Islamic leaders of that country more than the Left, which the United States had made sure was suppressed and crushed throughout the reign of the Shah, and even later as we will see. In other words, it was the United States' own policies that made a revolution, and specifically an Islamic revolution, both possible and probable.

As the great historian Eric Hobsbawm opined, "Still, in the 1960's and 1970's the old communist and National opposition was kept down by the secret police, regional and ethnic movements were repressed, as were the usual Leftist guerilla groups, whether orthodox Marxist or Islamic-Marxist. These could not provide the spark for the explosion. . . . The spark came from the peculiar specialty of the Iranian scene, the organized and politically active Islamic clergy which occupied a public position that had no real parallel elsewhere in the Muslim world, or even within its Shiite sector. . . ."[5]

Another phenomenon that led to the 1979 Revolution, and to the religious nature of it, was the decades-long repression of Iran's intellectuals by the Shah. Of course, there is an intersection between the repression of leftists and intellectuals as these two groups are many times, in truth, one and the same. And, even in instances where the overlap is not complete, they are often confused as the same.

Ryzard Kapuscinski, in his book *The Shah of Shahs*, eloquently explains how the repression of intellectuals *per se*, and how the very brutality of the repressive system in general, played a role in making the Islamic Revolution a near certainty.

As he states, the Shah, and I would argue also the United States which backed the Shah,

> left people a choice between Savak and the mullahs. And they chose the mullahs. When thinking about the fall of any dictatorship, one should have no illusions that the whole system comes to an end like a

bad dream with that fall. The physical existence of the system does indeed cease. But its psychological and social results live on for years, and even survive in the form of subconsciously continued behavior. A dictatorship that destroys the intelligentsia and culture leaves behind itself an empty, sour field on which the tree of thought won't grow quickly. It is not always the best people who emerge from hiding, from the corners and cracks of that farmed-out field, but often those who have proven themselves strongest, not always those who will create new values but rather those whose thick skin and internal resilience have ensured their survival. In such circumstances history begins to turn in a tragic, vicious circle from which it can sometimes take a whole epoch to break free.[6]

This point should be obvious: if one creates a system, which the Shah and his backer the United States surely did, that snuffs out the best and brightest of the nation, either through murder, imprisonment or exile, then how does one expect the best and the brightest to rise up to lead the nation after the dictatorship is brought down? Likewise, when one creates a barbaric torture state and keeps it in place for over a quarter of a century, why would anyone be surprised if something monstrous, or at least less than ideal, is borne from this?

Again, it is important to point out the double standard at work here. Thus, while many might recall how persecuted intellectuals in the Soviet Union, such as Andrei Sakharov and Alexandr Solzhenitsyn, became household names and symbols of all the was wrong in the USSR, who knew or cared about Iranian intellectuals who were jailed and tortured under the Shah?

A November 17, 1976, cable on WikiLeaks, for example, quotes a letter from a Congressman to the US secretary of state which focuses on Iran's greatest playwright who was still imprisoned after two years:

ENCLOSED IS A FACT SHEET ON THE CASE OF DR. GHOLAMHOSSEIN SA'EDI. DR. SA'EDI IS ONE OF IRAN'S LEADING

PLAYWRIGHTS AND A PROMINENT ANTHROPOLOGIST. I
UNDERSTAND THAT HE HAS BEEN IMPRISONED AND POS-
SIBLY TORTURED ON A NUMBER OF OCCASIONS BECAUSE
OF HIS WRITINGS. IT IS REPORTED THAT HE REMAINS
UNDER CONSTANT SURVELLIENCE AND HARRASSMENT
BY THE AGENTS OF SAVAK. DR. SA'EDI WOULD LIKE TO
LEAVE IRAN. I WOULD LIKE TO URGE THE DEPARTMENT
TO MAKE REPRESENTATIONS TO THE GOVERNMENT OF
IRAN TO ALLOW MR. SA'EDI TO LEAVE THE COUNTRY.
YOUR KIND ATTENTION TO THIS MATTER WILL BE
GREATLY APPRECIATED. END QUOTE.

FACT SHEET STATES SA'EDI IS "IRAN'S GREATEST
LIVING ... PLAYWRIGHT" AND ALSO WAS EDITOR OF LIT-
ERARY MAGAZINE ALEFBA. SAYS HE HAS BEEN IN PRISON
SINCE 1974 AND GOI HAS NOT MADE ANY INFORMATION
ABOUT THAT IMPRISONMENT PUBLIC. SHEET REVIEWS
SA'EDI'S WRITING CAREER AND MENTIONS OTHER
AUTHORS SUCH AS BARAHENI, ALI SHARIATTI, SAMAD
BEHRANGIE, KHOSROW GOLSORKHI AND KARAMAT
DANESHIAN, WHO ARE OR WERE IN PRISON.[7]

Why were not such writers and authors of Iran household names and
symbols of the Shah's depravity? Of course, the answer is clear:
because the Shah was "our boy," and therefore got a free pass. His
victims were not worthy, therefore, and sank into oblivion as a consequence. I am sure many Iranians noted our collective indifference to
their literary heroes, and remember our lack of caring still.

Meanwhile, in overturning the aged and kind Mossadegh, a leader
famous for conducting business in his bed and greeting foreign dignitar-
ies in his pink pajamas, the United States had actually taught the Islamic
revolutionaries that good guys finish last, and they took this to heart.

As Robert Fisk explains, "Mossadeq's rule and the coup that ended
Iran's independence in 1953 would provide a bitter lesson to the

revolutionaries of 1979. If the Shah was ever to be dethroned, there could be no flirtation with constitutional rights, no half-measures, no counter-revolutionaries left to restore Western power to Iran. A future revolution would embrace more than five thousand dead; it must be final, absolute—and unforgiving. The spies, the *ancien régime*, would have to be liquidated at once."[8]

Again, it is the utter lack of historical perspective that continues to doom US foreign policy, and the countries to which this policy is applied time and time again. I have compared the US view of history to the movie *Groundhog Day*, where somehow history begins anew and fresh each day without carrying with it the baggage from yesterday and the day before and the day before that. In the case of Iran, the CIA played midwife to a cruel system in 1953 which the Iranians have yet to fully break free from, and we as a nation must own up to this fact.

But of course, Americans are not good at all at owning up to the consequences of the suffering our nation has caused to others. And so, the United States has yet to apologize to Vietnam for the suffering we inflicted upon them during the war. Even more shocking, the United States still refuses to help them with the pain they continue to suffer in the form of land mines which the US military laid and which still explode there, or in the form of babies which continue to be born with horrible birth defects due to the napalm and Agent Orange the United States dumped on their country.

Similarly, we grind and gnash our teeth about the thousands of unaccompanied minors who risk life and limb and sexual abuse to enter the United States illegally, rarely stopping to consider what the United States did over the years to make their countries, such as El Salvador, Guatemala, and Honduras, uninhabitable through the death squad governments the US imposed upon them for so many years.

Again, this never happened as far as most of us are concerned, and if it did, it is not our problem now because the war is over. But for these countries, the effects of the war are not over, and they may not be over for many years to come. In the case of North Korea, what's more, the war itself has literally never ended as there was never a peace treaty signed between the warring parties. North Korea is painfully aware of this fact which, in addition to its being utterly levelled by the United States during the conflict, contributes to its defensiveness and paranoia.

In the case of Iran, moreover, what is not widely known is that the United States intervened in the final days of the Shah, who was cancer-stricken and whose reign was clearly at an end, to ensure that the successor government would be Islamic rather than leftist and secular, the latter being always anathema to the United States.

Thus, while Jimmy Carter had rejected pleas in November 1978 by his own ambassador to Iran, William Sullivan, to abandon the Shah, Carter changed course in late January of 1979 when keeping the Shah in power then seemed impossible due to Iranian public sentiment as well as the poor health of the Shah who had been diagnosed with terminal cancer.[9] At this point, Carter encouraged the Shah to leave the country. At the same time, he helped pave the way for the return of Imam Khomeini, who had been making conciliatory overtures to the United States as far back as the Kennedy years, from his exile in Paris.

Carter, whose other interest besides preventing a leftist government was the preservation of the Iranian military which the United States helped build up in the first place and which Carter wanted to continue as leverage in the Middle East, helped broker a deal between Khomeini and the Iranian military.[10] Specifically, with the help of US General Robert E. Huyser, Carter brokered a deal whereby the military, which was suspected of having its own coup plans, would stand down and allow the return and ascendancy of Khomeini in return for Khomeini's agreement to keep the military intact.

For his part, Khomeini, who courted the Carter Administration and who was in direct talks with the administration for a critical two weeks, also volunteered that he would make sure that Jews in Iran would be protected, and he would follow up with a Fatwah requiring that no harm be carried out against Iranian Jews.[11] Khomeini also assured the United States that he was happy to align against the atheistic USSR, which was of course music to ears of the Carter Administration and particularly to its hardcore Cold Warrior, National Security Adviser Zbigniew Brzezinski. And, as discussed above, Khomeini would immediately begin to violently purge Iran of Marxists and other leftists, again much to the delight of Washington.

None of this should be too surprising given the United States' long track record of working with radical religious groups to destroy the left. And indeed, there is evidence in recently-released CIA and MI6 documents that the United States worked with two ayatollahs in helping to overthrow Mossadegh in 1953, and made direct payments to at least one, if not both of them, to support their anti-Mossadegh agitation and organizing.[12]

And, even years after the 1979 Islamic Revolution in Iran, the United States worked closely with Khomeini in ensuring that the last vestiges of the left were wiped out in Iran.

As Christopher Davidson sets forth in his recent book, *Shadow Wars*, the United States and Britain continued to aid and abet Iran, even more intensely after the 1979 Islamic Revolution, in the physical extermination of Iran's left-wing. As Davidson explains, in 1983 "the CIA and MI6 jointly began to pass on information to the Tehran regime about Iranian communists and other leftists. Going far further than the Shah ever had, Khomeini made over a thousand arrests and executed several leaders of the *Tudeh* Party. As James Bill describes, this was regarded in the West as successfully 'completing the dismantling of the Iranian left,' even though the CIA and MI6 had long been aware of the Islamic Republic's propensity for executing political prisoners without trial."[13]

The brutal suppression of the *Tudeh* Party by the Khomeini government was particularly cruel given that this party, while weakened due to the Shah's longtime repression, nonetheless contributed to the uprising against the Shah, particularly with its leadership of the critical strikes in the oil sector which helped bring him down.[14]

Khomeini's paranoia about the Left at this time, and his consequent brutality against it, was heightened by the fact that he was
not only in the midst of a war with Iraq but was also confronting terrorist attacks being carried out by the MEK—a group which at least
claimed to be Marxist and which was being supported by Saddam
Hussein.

I have friends in Iran who are communists (of course underground) and they tell me that there are elements of the Iranian
government who are at least remorseful for the violent suppression of
the Iranian Left, and especially of the *Tudeh* Party, and that there are
public discussions about how to treat this past and how to treat the
Left in the future.

Of course, the United States and United Kingdom have always
tolerated, to the say the least, such human rights abuses against communists, socialists, and other leftists and therefore harbor absolutely
no remorse for the violent eradication of the Iranian Left. One other
example, among many others, is the mass slaughter of communists in
Indonesia, another predominantly Muslim country, after the US-backed
coup in that country in 1965. The slaughter against the members of the
communist PKI Party that followed the coup—a slaughter fully supported by the United States—cost the lives of between 500,000 and 1.2
million people.[15]

In the case of the Middle East, such Western-sponsored violence
against the Left has played no small role in the rise of Islamic
fundamentalism.

Meanwhile, the West, and the United States in particular, has
reaped a whirlwind as a result of their relentless and violent campaign
in the Middle East against the secular Left. The most notable example
of this was of course the 9/11 attacks. In the case of 9/11, however, it
must be emphasized that this was NOT carried out by Iran, or any
Shiite extremists, but rather was carried out (as far as we know) by
another, much worse monster created by horrible US foreign policies—
the radical Sunni group, al-Qaeda, led by Osama bin Laden.

Osama bin Laden was himself a Saudi, and, as we now know, al-Qaeda has received much support over the years from Saudi Arabia, the United States' longtime partner in crime in the Middle East and mortal enemy of Iran. Hillary Clinton herself acknowledged the Saudi (and Qatar) support for al-Qaeda, and ISIS as well, in a 2014 email leaked during her presidential bid.[16] Then Vice President Joe Biden also acknowledged the fact that there are not truly any "moderate rebels" in Syria, at least as of 2014, and that the support flowing to Syrian rebels from Saudi Arabia and Qatar (and the United States as well) has in fact been going to radical jihadists.[17]

In addition, as we learned from the infamous "twenty-eight pages" (really, twenty-nine) of the Congressional report on 9/11, Saudi Arabia provided substantial backing for the 9/11 attacks themselves.[18] This backing included financial support to some of the 9/11 hijackers from members of the Saudi royal family and intelligence services. FBI documents even show that the Saudi Embassy in Washington provided financial support for a "dry run" of the 9/11 operation.[19] Indeed, "Six years after the [9/11] attack, at the height of the military conflict in Iraq in 2007, Stuart Levey, the undersecretary of the US Treasury in charge of monitoring and impeding terror financing, told ABC News that, when it came to al-Qaeda, 'if I could somehow snap my fingers and cut off the funding of one country, it would be Saudi Arabia.'"[20]

And so, it stands to reason, the United States is a fierce ally of Saudi Arabia in its feud against Iran?!

Of course, al-Qaeda had its origins in the Mujahideen which the United States armed and funded in order to fatally undermine the secular, left-wing government then in power in Afghanistan, and to weaken the USSR in the process. Osama bin Laden, the young radical Saudi, was one of the leaders in the Mujahideen forces, and then an ally of the United States and recipient of US largesse. Contrary to popular opinion, the United States did not arm these forces in order to counter the Soviet invasion of Afghanistan, but rather, to bring about such an invasion.

Thus, as then US National Security Adviser Zbigniew Brzezinski later admitted, the arming of the Mujahideen began in July of 1979—six months BEFORE the Soviet invasion, and very shortly after the overthrow of the Shah of Iran in February of that year.

Brzezinski would later quip that the arming of the Mujahideen had the intended "effect of drawing the Russians into the Afghan trap and you want me to regret it? The day that the Soviets officially crossed the border, I wrote to President Carter. We now have the opportunity of giving to the USSR its Vietnam war."[21]

When asked about whether he regretted the rise of Islamic extremism which followed in the wake of the US-Mujahideen operations, Brzezinski was nonplussed, replying, "What is more important in world history? The Taliban or the collapse of the Soviet empire? Some agitated Moslems or the liberation of Central Europe and the end of the cold war?" Brzezinski expressed this sentiment in 1998, a few years before 9/11.

After the 9/11 attacks, the United States quickly attacked the Taliban government in Afghanistan—a government which directly grew out of the Mujahideen forces which the United States sponsored to draw the Soviet Union into a brutal war in Afghanistan, and which was allied with al-Qaeda and Osama bin Laden himself. Iran, a mortal enemy of the Taliban and the Sunni radicals, offered to assist the United States in this effort and gave such assistance.

Meanwhile, after the Iran-Iraq war ended, and US ally Saddam Hussein had done his worst against the Iranians, the United States quickly decided that he was not a reliable enough ally, and therefore invaded Iraq in 1991, imposed brutal economic sanctions upon the Iraqi people, and intermittently bombed Iraq through the 1990s.

9

A TALE OF TWO REVOLUTIONS— IRAN AND NICARAGUA

Several months after the Shah was overthrown in Iran, and in the very same month that the United States began funding the Mujahideen in Afghanistan, the people of Nicaragua overthrew a US-backed dictator of their own named Anastasio Somoza. There are many parallels and intersections between these two revolutions which make looking at the Nicaraguan revolution, and how the United States has responded to it, worthwhile.

Unlike Iran—a fairly large country, indeed the seventeenth largest in the world, with sizable oil reserves—Nicaragua is a small country with nearly no coveted resources to speak of. And, at the time of the 1979 revolution, Nicaragua had less than three million people as compared to Iran's population of forty million.

Still, the United States has had its eye on Nicaragua, a country with both a Pacific and Atlantic coast, for a long time in part because of its huge lake (Lake Nicaragua) which could be transformed into a canal for shipping much larger than the Panama Canal, the latter canal being violently stolen from Colombia in 1903 by Kermit's grandfather, Teddy

Roosevelt. Indeed, in 1914, the United States bought the rights to build the Nicaraguan canal for $3 million. This $3 million also bought them the leasing rights to two Nicaraguan islands as well as the right to build a naval base in the Gulf of Fonseca.

The problem was that the Nicaraguans are a quite proud and independent people, and they bristled over the United States' attempts to control their country. The Nicaraguans would therefore rise up in protest often against US intervention. In response, the United States began militarily intervening in Nicaragua in 1912, sending in the Marines periodically to quell opposition. However, every time the Marines would withdraw, the people would rise up again. And so, in 1927, the Marines began to occupy Nicaragua.

Not too surprisingly, the Nicaraguans were quite unhappy about the presence of foreign troops on their soil and about being declared a "protectorate of the United States." One brave Nicaraguan, Augusto Cesar Sandino, organized a band of guerillas to attack and molest the Marines, and he was quite successful in doing so. Indeed, Sandino would lead about five hundred attacks on the Marines who were never able to defeat Sandino or to even find where he and his band of merry men were hiding.

In 1933 the United States, now really desperate, would try out some of the world's first aerial bombings against Sandino's guerillas as well as the sympathetic, rural Nicaraguan population. By the way, it may be interesting to some to know that the Wright brothers actually believed that the only viable commercial use for their airplane invention would be for just such military purposes, and they indeed marketed the airplane in keeping with this belief, including to the US War Department.[1] Here were the beginnings of the military-industrial complex.

Notwithstanding the United States' much superior fire power, Sandino and his forces would successfully oust the Marines in 1934.

However, before leaving Nicaragua, the US Marines helped to set up the brutal National Guard (*Guardia Nacional*) to maintain order in

Nicaragua in their stead. The United States installed a man named Anastasio Somoza Garcia as the head of the National Guard in 1934. Unable to defeat Sandino, Somoza lured Sandino to the capital, Managua, with the promise of a peace accord and had him assassinated.

In 1936, with Sandino out of the way, Anastasio Somoza Garcia, with the full backing of the United States, became the dictatorial ruler of Nicaragua. It was of Somoza that President Franklin D. Roosevelt remarked, "He is a son-of-a-bitch, but he is our son-of-bitch." With the strong backing of the United States, Anastasio Somoza Garcia, his son, and then his grandson would rule Nicaragua with an iron hand continuously until the 1979 Revolution.

One might pause here to wonder how it is that the United States claims to support democracy and freedom in the world when it so often backs dictators like the Shah and Somoza. As I tell my human rights class every year, the United States always supports democracy and freedom, except when it doesn't, which is all the time. . . .

As political analyst Stephen Gowans explains, the United States is simply not what it claims to be, and most likely never has been:

The United States—which began as 13 former British colonies on the Atlantic coast of North America pursuing a "manifest destiny" of continental expansion, (the inspiration for Nazi Germany's *lebensraum* policy); which fought a war with Spain for colonies; which promulgated the Monroe Doctrine asserting a sphere of influence in the Americas; which stole Panama to create a canal; whose special operations forces project US power in 81 countries; whose generals control the militaries of the combined NATO members in Europe and the military forces of South Korea; whose military command stations one hundred thousand troops on the territories of former imperialist rivals, manifestly has an empire. And yet this reality is denied, as assuredly as is the reality that the United States, built on the genocide of Native Americans and the slave labor of Africans, overtly white supremacist until the mid-1960s, and covertly white supremacist since, is unequivocally *not* a beacon of Enlightenment values, unless liberalism is defined as equality and liberty assigned exclusively to white men who own productive property. Indeed, so antithetical is the United States to the liberal values of the equality of all peoples and nations, freedom from exploitation and oppression, and the absence of discrimination on the bases of class, race, and sex, that it's difficult to apprehend in what sense the United States has ever been liberal or has in any way had a legitimate claim to being the repository of the values of the Enlightenment.[2]

Certainly, the Nicaraguans must wonder the very same about such US pretensions.

In the case of Nicaragua, the dictatorship would not hold, notwithstanding the best efforts of the United States, and its usual partner in crime, Israel, to keep it in power. And, as is often the case, the dictatorship demonstrated its worst brutality in its final death throes. As Noam Chomsky so well explains in his book, *What Uncle Sam Really Wants*:

When his rule was challenged by the Sandinistas [the insurgent group named after Augusto Cesar Sandino] in the late 1970s, the US first tried to institute what was called "Somocismo [Somoza-ism] without Somoza"- that is, the whole corrupt system intact, but with somebody else at the top. That didn't work, so President Carter tried to maintain Somoza's National Guard as a base for US power.

The National Guard had always been remarkably brutal and sadistic. By June 1979, it was carrying out massive atrocities in the war against the Sandinistas, bombing residential neighborhoods in Managua, killing tens of thousands of people. At that point, the US ambassador sent a cable to the White House saying it would be "ill advised" to tell the Guard to call off the bombing, because that might interfere with the policy of keeping them in power and the Sandinistas out.

Our ambassador to the Organization of American States also spoke in favor of "Somocismo without Somoza," but the OAS rejected the suggestion flat out. A few days later, Somoza flew off to Miami with what was left of the Nicaraguan national treasury, and the Guard collapsed.

The Carter administration flew Guard commanders out of the country in planes with Red Cross markings (a war crime), and began to reconstitute the Guard on Nicaragua's borders. They also used Argentina as a proxy. (At that time, Argentina was under the rule of neo-Nazi generals, but they took a little time off from torturing and murdering their own population to help reestablish the Guard -- soon to be renamed the contras, or "freedom fighters.")[3]

Again, we see Jimmy Carter not really living up to all of his lofty human rights rhetoric.

Unable to forgive the Nicaraguans for ousting one of their beloved dictators, just as it could not forgive the Iranians for the same offense, the United States would then back these Contra forces throughout the 1980s.

While Ronald Reagan would refer to the Contras as the "moral equivalent of our Founding Fathers," this did not reflect so well on our Founding Fathers. For example, an *LA Times* article from 1985 cited the International Human Rights Law Group who documented "a pattern of brutality against largely unarmed civilians, including rape, torture, kidnappings, mutilation and other abuses" by the Contra forces. As just one example of this, the *LA Times* related the following account:

Children Slain

Typical among them was an Oct. 28, 1982, contra attack on the rural area of El Jicaro in northern Nicaragua. In an affidavit, Maria Bustillo, 57, testified that five armed men dressed in the FDN's blue uniforms burst into her house and dragged away her husband

Ricardo, a Roman Catholic activist, and five of their children. The next morning she found the mutilated bodies of the children. Her husband's body was found later.[4]

In addition to funding and training the Contras, the United States would also mine Nicaragua's harbors. And, the United States did so without even informing its allies who regularly anchored there. The International Court of Justice (ICJ) later found in the case of *Nicaragua v. United States* (1986) that because "neither before the laying of the mines, nor subsequently, did the United States government issue any public and official warning to international shipping of the existence and location of the mines . . . vessels of the Dutch, Panamanian, Soviet, Liberian and Japanese registry . . . were damaged by the mines. . . ."[5] The ICJ, which concluded that President Reagan had personally ordered this mining operation, found the callousness of the United States toward such third-party countries particularly reprehensible.

The ICJ found that the United States violated international law in its bilateral treaties with Nicaragua through the mining of the harbors, various other terrorist attacks such as the destruction of Nicaragua's oil storage facilities and pipelines, and through the funding and training of the Contras. As for the training, the ICJ, based upon the affidavit of Contra leader Edgar Chamorro, found that "training was at the outset provided by [fascist] Argentine military officers, paid by the CIA, gradually replaced by CIA personnel" who took over the training themselves.[6]

According to Chamorro, the CIA trained the Contras in "guerilla warfare, sabotage, demolitions, and in the use of a variety of weapons. . . ." Chamorro described the CIA officials as more than advisers to the Contras. Rather, they were the leaders of the group, with Chamorro attributing "virtually a power of command to the CIA operatives." The ICJ found that, under the CIA's direction and control, the Contras carried out numerous incidents of "kidnapping, assassinations, torture, rape, killing of prisoners, and killing of civilians not dictated by military necessity."[7]

In addition, the ICJ found that the United States violated international law norms through the CIA's *Psychological Operations in Guerilla Warfare* manual which, among other things, advised the Contra forces to organize people for public executions. Specifically, the manual called for "Selective Use of Violence for Propagandistic Effects" in which "selected and planned targets, such as court judges, *mesta* judges, police and State Security officials, CDS chiefs, etc." would be "neutralize[d]" by a particular population which "will be present, [and] take part in the act" of killing the target.[8]

The United States not only disregarded the ICJ's judgment—pursuant to which Nicaragua estimated it was owed nearly $400 million in compensation—but also declared that it was no longer subject to ICJ jurisdiction at all unless it explicitly consented to such for a particular case. Justice is, after all, to be administered against the weak, not the strong.

The atrocities of the Contras became such a problem that the US Congress ended up cutting off their funding through legislation known as The Boland Amendment. Undeterred, the Reagan Administration found creative ways to continue arming and bankrolling the Contras, nonetheless.

In addition to funding the Contras through illicit sales of cocaine, with at least $14 million in drug sales being used as seed money to fund the post-Boland Amendment arms trade to the Contras,[9] the Reagan Administration would also turn to Iran to aid its scheme. The problem there was that the United States was then supporting Iraq in its war against Iran, and there was therefore an arms embargo against Iran at this time. Again, Reagan would find a way.

Nothing but total capitulation by the Sandinistas would suffice for Reagan. Thus, as the ICJ related, revolutionary leader and then Nicaraguan president Daniel Ortega made it clear that he would give in to all of Reagan's stated demands (i.e., that he would send home the

Cuban and Russians advisers and not support the FMLN guerillas in El Salvador) in return for only "one thing: that they don't attack us, that the United States stop arming and financing . . . the gangs that kill our people, burn our crops and force us to divert enormous human and economic resources into war when we desperately need them for development."[10] But Reagan would not relent until the Sandinistas and Ortega were out of power altogether.

Ultimately, Reagan's terror campaign would work, with the Nicaraguan people finally crying uncle in 1990, and voting the Sandinistas out of power. The Sandinistas would be voted back in, however, in 2007, and they remain the governing party to this day, with Daniel Ortega as president.

Meanwhile, the United States continues to punish Nicaragua, the most stable and prosperous country in Central America after successfully breaking off from US domination, for its impertinence in overthrowing the Somoza dictatorship, having the audacity to survive the Contra War which claimed fifty thousand lives, voting back in the Sandinistas, and for now working with the Chinese to build the canal that the United States has coveted for so long. Thus, as I write these lines, the US Senate is considering passage of the "Nica Act," already passed by the House, which would cut Nicaragua off from multilateral loans (e.g., from the World Bank, IMF). This, apparently, will show Nicaragua and other countries what they get for deciding to go their own way.

THE IRAN-IRAQ WAR— PLAYING BOTH SIDES AGAINST EACH OTHER

THE TRUTH ABOUT THE UNITED STATES' engagement in the Middle East over the past seventy years or so must be baffling to most Americans, at least to the extent that they are aware of it, as there appears to be little sanity in the entire arch of US involvement in the region.

Thus, to the extent that Iran currently has an Islamic government which the United States and Israel seem to abhor, it is directly a consequence of the US coup against Prime Minister Mohammad Mossadegh in 1953, its subsequent support of the Shah and the dreaded SAVAK security forces which made popular revolt inevitable and the United States' direct support of the Islamists in Iran over the secular left.

Still, the United States, in line with its usual habit of attacking the regimes which it has helped make possible or even installed, moved quickly to try to destroy the Islamic Republic. Analogous to its brutal Contra war against the recalcitrant nation of Nicaragua, the United States supported a vicious war against Iran very shortly after the ousting of the Shah. And, the United States turned to its old friend Saddam Hussein to wage this war.

The war between Iran and Iraq began with the Iraqi invasion of Iran in September 1980. Even as war between Iran and Iraq appeared imminent, with military skirmishes from both sides on the frontier, the UN Security Council refused to act. And, when Iraq invaded Iran, the UN Security Council would not even call upon Iraq to withdraw its troops. As Robert Fisk relates, "Iran was convinced that the whole world now turned against its revolution and was supporting the act of aggression by Saddam."[1] Of course, Iran was absolutely correct.

The world, and quite notably the Western world, remained silent when Iraq, feeling frustrated with the lack of an easy and quick victory which it had anticipated against the new revolutionary government in Iran, resorted to crueler and crueler methods.

First, Iraq attempted to deal with its being greatly outnumbered by the "human waves" of Iranians confronting its forces. According to journalist Mohamad Salam, Iraq began using a tactic which it first used in the three towns located in the Howeiza marshes of Iran. Salam describes the operation as such:

> [Iraqi Major General Hisham Sabah] Al-Fakhry brought huge tanker trucks down and pumped fuel into the marshland and then fired incendiary shells into the water and started the biggest fire I've seen in my entire life. He burned and killed everything, the whole environment.
>
> Then, when the fire was out, he brought electrical generators and put huge cables into the marsh waters and electrified everything so that there was no source of life left in that place. . . .
>
> Gutted bodies were floating everywhere, even women and children were among them—marsh people, people who knew what a toad was, people who'd lived among ducks and buffaloes and fished with spears, this civilization was being wiped out. I saw about thirty women and children, all gutted open like fish, and many, many Iranians. The innocent had to die along with the living.[2]

When Saddam became even more desperate, he announced that he would destroy Iran's "human waves" another way, but he did not refer to these waves as "human." As he announced over the radio in 1985, "The waves of insects are attacking the eastern gates of the Arab Nation. But I have the pesticides to wipe them out." In one attack alone, Saddam would kill at least 4,700 Iranians with "a blistering agent that damages all human tissues."[3]

While this was the first massive chemical weapons use of its kind since WWI, the West, and its ever-compliant press, was either silent or dismissive of the Iranians' claims of chemical weapons use by Hussein.

I note that this was the first use of such chemical weapons "of its kind" since WWI because the United States of course used more modern chemical weapons such as napalm and Agent Orange on a massive scale during the Korean and Vietnam wars as well as against peasants in Colombia in the mid-1960s. This fact is often overlooked, including by *The Nonproliferation Review* itself which I cite extensively here and which simply says, without caveat, that Iraq's use of chemical weapons during this war was the first use of any chemical weapons since WWI. This is simply not true, but it is certainly revealing of the incredible denial in the West, including amongst people who should know better, of our own great criminality in war.

Of course, it was the West itself, and specifically Germany and the United States, which supplied Saddam Hussein with his chemical weapons and technology for making more. Thus, a US Senate Committee would finally inform Congress in 1994 that the United States had been providing Iraq with biological and chemical agents, which could be weaponized, since 1985 when Saddam had made his vow to use "pesticides" to wipe out the Iranian "insects."[4] The biological agents provided included anthrax and E. coli. Along with these agents, the United States generously provided technical drawings for a chemical production plant along with "chemical warhead filling equipment."

In addition, it is known that Saddam was importing chemicals for weapons use, such as one thousand tons of thiodiglycol, a key component of mustard gas, from Western Europe and the United States at an even earlier date.[5] Iraq began to use mustard gas regularly in the war with Iran by 1983.

In a damning report by US Senator Donald Riegle in 1994, based in part upon the UN weapons inspections which took place in Iraq after the First Gulf War, Riegle explained:

> UN inspectors had identified many United States manufactured items that had been exported from the United States to Iraq under licenses issued by the Department of Commerce, and [established] that these items were used to further Iraq's chemical and nuclear weapons development and its missile delivery system development programs. . . . The executive branch of our government approved 771 different export licenses of dual-use technology to Iraq. I think that is a devastating record.[6]

According to the Riegle Report, as it is typically called, the US Centers for Disease Control sent Iraq fourteen separate agents "with biological warfare significance."[7] In this instance, the CDC was not so much involved in controlling disease, but rather, spreading it.

Moreover, in addition to supplying the deadly chemical weapons to Iraq, the United States, throughout the war, provided Iraq "with battlefield intelligence so that they could prepare themselves for the mass Iranian attacks and defend themselves—as the US government knew—with poison gas."[8] In the end, according to Iran's official tally, 60,000 Iranians were killed in chemical attacks by Iraq during the course of the war, out of a total of 500,000 to 600,000 total Iranians killed during the conflict.[9]

And, of course, Saddam Hussein did not reserve chemical weapons use just for the Iranians, but for his own Kurds, bombarding the Iraqi town of Halabjah for three days with US- and German-supplied chemicals, killing five to eight thousand people, "including Kurdish civilians (mostly women, children, and the elderly). . . ." in the process.[10]

To add insult to injury, some in the US government and media attempted to blame Iran somehow for this attack when it had nothing to do with it.

To the contrary, it must be emphasized that Iran, while having some chemical weapons capability of its own at the time, never retaliated against Iraq in kind for its chemical weapons attacks even though international law, and specifically the reservations to the 1925 Geneva Protocol,[11] would have allowed for such retaliation.

Indeed, during the height of the war and of the suffering being inflicted upon Iran by Saddam's chemical weapons attacks, Ayatollah Khomeini made clear his view that Islamic law, which forbids the willful destruction of the environment, necessarily prohibits the development and use of chemical weapons.[12] He made it clear, therefore, that Iran would not use such weapons against Iraq even though Saddam was using such weapons, and the available evidence supports the conclusion that Khomeini lived by his word.

Later, in 2005, the Ayatollah Ali Khamenei would issue a Fatwah against the production, stockpiling, and use of nuclear weapons as inimical to the Islamic faith. The foregoing "strongly suggests that the Iranian leadership's aversion to developing chemical and nuclear weapons is deep-rooted and sincere."[13]

This also strongly suggests that Iran's ayatollahs may in fact not be the madmen and villains that we are led every day to believe they are. In fact, our own leaders seem much madder in comparison.

More proof of the relative and absolute insanity of our leaders is that the United States armed Iran at the very same time it was aiding Iraq in the war effort in return for payment which it used to illegally fund the Contra terrorists after Congress had cut off aid to them. Later known as the Iran-Contra Scandal, the CIA would secretly sell Iran more than 1500 TOW missiles in return for $30 million—$18 million of which would go to the Contras.[14]

In addition to its motive to find funding for the Contras, the United States, along with Israel, also aided both sides of the Iran-Iraq

conflict in a cynical move to try to weaken both countries with a protracted war. For its part, Israel sold Iran hundreds of millions of dollars
of US-manufactured weapons during the Iran-Iraq war—Israel claims
with full US consent and approval—and by all accounts assisted Iran
in keeping up its end of the fighting, especially in the initial years of
the war.[15] The arms sold to Iran by Israel included Lance missiles, Cop-
perhead shells, Hawk missiles, submachine guns, anti-tank missile
launchers, howitzers, and aircraft replacement parts.[16]

Such a cynical plan was nothing new in the 1980s, and this plan
indeed continues to be played out by the United States today.

As Christopher Davidson points out in *Shadow Wars*, "In many
ways, the West's position . . . is reminiscent of Harry Truman's views
on Nazi Germany before the US entered the Second World War. After
all, as his well-documented remarks on Adolf Hitler's invasion of the
Soviet Union reveal, he and others did not really want to see either side
winning, while any long-drawn-out fight between the two sides was
seen as ultimately suiting US interests."[17] Indeed, it is noteworthy to
recall that the United States did not enter the European theater with
full force during WWII until its D-Day invasion of Normandy on June
4, 1944—that is, just shy of three years after the Soviet Union had been
invaded by Germany on June 22, 1941, and well after the Soviets had
forced the Germans to start their retreat back to Berlin with the Red
Army in hot pursuit. Millions of lives had been lost as a result of the
United States' delay.

Davidson explains that, similarly, "in the Middle East itself, the
desire for such similarly balanced conflicts is of course nothing new,
with the Iran-Iraq War of the 1980s having helped cancel out the two
major powers of the day. . . ." Davidson cites William Blum for the
proposition that the West's support of both sides of the Iran-Iraq war
"had the effect of 'enhancing the ability of the two countries to inflict
maximum devastation upon each other and stunt their growth as
strong Middle East nations'." In the words of the *New York Times*, the

goal was "to prolong the slaughter and so weaken both countries, along with their ability to oppose US domination of the region."[18]

As Davidson and others have noted, the United States is continuing this cruel policy of playing both sides against each other today by supporting, but also trying to contain, ISIS forces in order to molest and undermine both Syria and Iran; by intentionally stirring up religious sectarianism in the Middle East, and in particular, animosities between the Shia and the Sunnis; and by playing Saudi Arabia against Iran.

Meanwhile, the United States' efforts to keep the Iran and Iraq war going as long as possible were quite successful. As *History.com* notes, this war "was inordinately protracted, lasting longer than either world war. . . ."[19] The result of the eight-year war between Iran and Iraq was the death of around one million people total on both sides of the bloody conflict—a conflict which the Western press barely bothered to cover at all.

But the painful memories of this war linger in the minds of Iranians. Indeed, "The memory of the eight-year Iran-Iraq War in the 1980s shapes Iran's outlook on the Arab world. Many senior Iranian leaders are veterans of that war, during which Iraq annexed Iranian territory, used chemical weapons against Iranian troops, and terrorized Iranian cities with missile attacks."[20] No wonder that Iran feels constantly on the defensive against hostile forces.

Meanwhile, though Iraq was weakened during the eight-year conflict with Iran, it was not weakened quite enough as far as US policy-makers were concerned. Therefore, the United States invaded Iraq three years later, and then finished the job in 2003 with a second invasion which left the country in shambles.

Incredibly, the United States, knowing no shame, justified the 2003 war with the claim that Iraq at that time, still being led by Saddam Hussein, possessed "weapons of mass destruction" (WMDs)—in particular, banned chemical weapons. Of course, that turned out to be untrue, as Hussein's chemical weapons store had been destroyed under UN supervision years before. However, as with every other war of choice the United States has involved itself in since WWII—and they have all been wars of choice—the press was quite happy to disseminate the lies about WMDs.

No better example of this was our great "paper of record," the *New York Times*, whose "journalist" Judith Miller provided the Bush Administration with the alibi it needed for the invasion it so desperately wanted. Thus, relying upon dubious sources who themselves were trying to push us into war—one of whom, Ahmed Chalabi, was the very same source the White House was relying upon, and another source who she never met or interviewed herself—Miller published "evidence" of WMDs, including bogus claims about Saddam allegedly attempting to pursue nuclear weapons, which the White House itself would point to as corroboration of its own WMD claims.[21] In short, she collaborated with the White House in creating a perfect echo chamber of lies which led to a war which has cost this country trillions of dollars and which has cost over one million Iraqi lives. Miller was certainly not the only journalist pushing such war propaganda.

But beyond that, there was an obvious hypocrisy to the WMD claim, for if Hussein had still possessed chemical weapons, they would have been weapons which the United States provided him during the height of its war against Iran. Indeed, as Robert Fisk explains, Donald Rumsfeld, who as secretary of defense under George W. Bush helped push for and then lead the 2003 invasion of Iraq, "made his notorious 1983 visit to Baghdad to shake Saddam's hand" even while Iraq was using chemical weapons, many made in America, to kill tens of thousands of Iranians.[22]

Another amazing justification for the 2003 invasion was not just that Hussein allegedly still had chemical weapons, but that he had used them against his own Kurdish population. Again, that is true, but he did so with the complicity of the United States, which had absolutely no problem with this attack at the time. But again, do not bother to look for consistency, truth, or morality in US foreign policy. Also, do not look for justice to be exacted against US officials involved in such crimes. Saddam Hussein's execution, largely justified on the basis of the gassing of the Kurds, is a perfect illustration of this fact, for if justice were meted out equally in this world, there would have been several Americans hanging alongside him for the same offense.

Fisk explains that "for all these years—until his invasion of Kuwait in 1990—we in the West tolerated Saddam's cruelty, his oppression and torture, his war crimes and murder. After all, we helped to create him. The CIA gave the locations of communist cadres to the first Ba'thist government, information that was used to arrest, torture, and execute hundreds of Iraqi men. And the closer Saddam came to the war with Iran, the greater his fear of his own Shia population, the more we helped him."[23] It should be pointed out, moreover, that many believe that Saddam felt comfortable invading Kuwait in 1990 because of the lack of US and international response, much less condemnation, of his crimes, including chemical weapons use, during the Iran-Iraq war.[20]

For the coup de grace, the United States would itself use chemical weapons (i.e., white phosphorous and depleted uranium) in its war on Iraq in 2003, causing spikes in cancer rates and birth defects in such heavily-targeted areas as Fallujah.[21]

* * *

When I think of the staggering numbers of victims of Saddam's chemical use, and of the United States' own chemical weapons use as well, combined with the near-total silence of US government officials and US journalists when these victims were losing their lives in the most cruel way, I can't help but think about the very different reaction to the alleged chemical attacks in Syria—attacks which have, by all accounts, claimed many fewer lives.

In addition, the poor and one-sided coverage of such events (e.g., with some of the press even claiming at the time that Iran was somehow responsible for Saddam's attack against the Kurds) makes me quite wary of all press coverage of foreign affairs. Again, the Syrian chemical attack coverage, which is aimed at vilifying Syria's ally Iran as much as Syria itself, comes to mind. Thus, the Western press has simply treated it as a truism that the Syrian government has carried out chemical attacks on its population when there is certainly good evidence that it is the US-backed rebels who have done so.[22]

As writer and long-time peace activist Rick Sterling recently opined, the chemical attacks in 2013 in Syria, which suspiciously happened just when UN observers were in Damascus, demonstrate the mainstream media's bias on such issues:

> In August of 2013 we heard about a massive sarin gas attack on the outskirts of Damascus. Human Rights Watch and others promoting a western attack quickly accused the Syrian government. They asserted that Assad had crossed Obama's "red line" and the US needed to intervene directly. Subsequent investigations revealed the gas attack was not carried out by the Syrian government. It was perpetrated by a Turkish supported terrorist faction with the goal of pressuring the Obama administration to directly attack Syria. Two Turkish parliamentarians presented evidence of Turkey's involvement in the transfer of sarin. Some of the best and most time-proven US investigative journalists, including Robert Parry and Seymour Hersh, researched and discovered the evidence points to Turkish supported "rebels" not Syria. Despite the factual evidence exposing the "junk heap" of false claims, mainstream media and their followers continue to assert that Assad committed the crime.[23]

At the time of this alleged chemical attack, Donald Trump tweeted out what was a reasonable note of caution to Obama, stating, "The only reason President Obama wants to attack Syria is to save face over his very dumb RED LINE statement. Do NOT attack Syria, fix U.S.A." In the end, it appears that Obama himself was ultimately convinced that Syria did not carry out this attack given what appeared to be his sudden about-face on attacking Syria just as he seemed poised to do it. Even this, however, did not move the press to modify its original coverage.

Similarly, the allegations about Assad's use of chemical weapons in early 2017, which precipitated Trump's bombing of targets outside Damascus—a bombing he carried out in contravention of his own, earlier advice to Obama—fell apart rather quickly. Thus, according to Colonel Lawrence Wilkerson, the former chief of staff for Secretary of State Colin Powell, a number of US intelligence sources concluded that Russia's claims about the alleged chemical attack were correct— that is, that what appeared to be a chemical attack was the result of the Russian conventional bombing of an ISIS warehouse which turned out to have chemicals stashed in it.[24] The Russians had even informed the US military of its intention to bomb this warehouse in advance. Wilkerson went so far as to characterize the claims of a Syrian chemical attack as a "hoax"—a hoax nonetheless swallowed hook, line, and sinker by the mainstream press.

And now, as I write these words in April of 2018, we are told of another alleged chemical attack in Syria. True to form, this alleged attack is said to have occurred just days after Trump announced that he had informed the US military to prepare to leave Syria altogether. The newest allegations, in addition to leading the United States to launch a missile attack against Syria, will also predictably serve as justification for the United States to continue its presence in Syria for the foreseeable future. In addition, this has served as a pretext for Israel to attack Iranian targets in Syria. Few, however, dare to ask whether this alleged attack was just too suspiciously convenient for the purposes of keeping the United States in a war which many in power seem to so desperately want.

But again, even putting aside whether or not Syria has carried out chemical attacks as alleged, the histrionics shown toward the alleged attacks comes off to me as selective, hypocritical, and just downright phony.

11

THE UNITED STATES, IRAN, AND THE TALIBAN

RECENTLY, PRESIDENT TRUMP ANNOUNCED THAT HE would be sending more troops to Afghanistan, and that we would be staying in that country indefinitely. Apparently, his decision to up the ante in Afghanistan was encouraged by his being shown a famous picture by former National Security Advisor H.R. McMaster of women walking freely down a street in Kabul wearing miniskirts and with books in hand[1]— the message being that we had to help Afghanistan return to such days when women had rights. Of course, what he was not told was that the photo was taken in 1972 when the Marxist and Soviet-allied government was in power in Afghanistan.

It was the United States, as mentioned elsewhere in this book, which ousted that government by supporting Islamic extremist guerilla forces known as the Mujahideen, who would ultimately topple the secular government in Afghanistan and become the new, Taliban government. It was the Taliban government, initially backed by the United States well into 2001, who would suppress the very women's rights the US government now claims it wants back in Afghanistan.

That is, it was the United States which played a key role in taking the rights away from women in Afghanistan. But Trump, apparently ignorant of such history, was easily manipulated, never questioning whether the United States had any credibility in claiming to be the protector of women's rights in Afghanistan. Sadly, Trump is not the only American ignorant of the quite recent past, and, unless we get up to speed on our history, we are sadly doomed to repeat it.

Even before taking power in Afghanistan, the US-supported Mujahideen forces, which included Osama bin Laden, were helping to roll back human rights in Afghanistan. Thus, in the name of fighting for freedom, they "murdered teachers, doctors, and nurses, tortured women for not wearing the veil and shot down civilian airliners with US-made Stinger missiles."[2]

But all is apparently fair in Cold War politics and the pursuit of oil. As for the latter interest, oil was and is a key reason for the US interest in Afghanistan, as it has been in neighboring Iran, and it is the reason we may never leave Afghanistan.

Few may remember that the United States was not only playing ball with the Taliban until just shortly before 9/11, but was in fact helping to bankroll it. And the reason was the desire to help Unocal (now Chevron) fulfill its dream of running a pipeline from the Caspian Sea region through Afghanistan and into Asia.[3]

As Central Asian expert Ahmed Rashid explains, " 'Impressed by the ruthlessness of the then-emerging Taliban to cut a pipeline deal, the [US] State Department and Pakistan's Inter-Services Intelligence agency agreed [back in 1994] to funnel arms and funding to the Taliban in their war against the ethnically Tajik North Alliance. As recently as 1999, US taxpayers paid the entire salary of every single Taliban government official,' " though the Taliban was not even recognized by the United Nations as the government of Afghanistan.[4]

The United States continued to aid the Taliban, pledging a total of $124 million in aid to the Taliban in early 2001, just several months before 9/11.[5] However, when negotiations between the United States and the Taliban began to sour over the pipeline project, the United States threatened to "carpet bomb" Afghanistan.[6] Finally, the United

States decided to invade Afghanistan even prior to 9/11 in light of the impasse over the oil pipeline, telling both India and Pakistan in early 2001 that they planned to invade Afghanistan in October. *Jane's Defense Newsletter* reported as early as March 2001 that the United States was planning such an invasion.[7]

Of course, the *casus belli* for the Afghan invasion came with the 9/11 attacks and the claim that the Taliban was "harboring" Osama bin Laden, though he would not remain in Afghanistan for very long and was ultimately found in Pakistan. Meanwhile, the Taliban made it clear that it would happily turn bin Laden over to the United States if it simply provided evidence that bin Laden was indeed behind the 9/11 attacks. The United States, unconcerned with such trifles as due process, refused this offer and went ahead with the invasion as it had intended to even before 9/11.

In truth, it should be noted that the United States could never have complied with the Taliban's request for evidence anyway, or at least not sufficient evidence, as even the FBI would have to admit. Thus, it was reported in 2006 that while the FBI listed bin Laden on its "Most Wanted List," the FBI did not include the 9/11 attacks as a basis for this listing. When asked why, Rex Tomb, then the FBI's chief of investigative publicity, admitted, "The reason why 9/11 is not mentioned on Usama Bin Laden's Most Wanted page is because the FBI has no hard evidence connecting Bin Laden to 9/11."[8]

In any case, the United States was late to the party, for Iran, along with Russia, had already been busy fighting the Taliban. Iran and Russia both would continue to fight the Taliban and to aid in the fight against al-Qaeda after 9/11.

In terms of Iran specifically, a CBS/AP article explains that

Iran rounded up hundreds of Arabs to help the United States counter al Qaeda after the Sept. 11 attack after they crossed the border from Afghanistan. . . . Many were expelled . . . and the Iranians made copies of almost 300 of their passports. The copies were sent to Kofi

Annan, then the secretary-general of the United Nations, who passed them to the United States, and U.S. interrogators were given a chance by Iran to question some of the detainees.

[Hillary Mann] Leverett, a Middle East expert who was a career U.S. Foreign Service officer, said she negotiated with Iran for the Bush administration in the 2001-3 period, and Iran sought a broader relationship with the United States. "They thought they had been helpful on al Qaeda, and they were" . . .

For one thing, she said, Iran denied sanctuary to suspected al Qaeda operatives. . . .

James F. Dobbins, the Bush administration's chief negotiator on Afghanistan in late 2001, said Iran was "comprehensively helpful" in the aftermath of the 9-11 attack in 2001 in working to overthrow the Taliban militias' rule and collaborating with the United States to install the Karzai government in Kabul.

Iranian diplomats made clear at the time they were looking for broader cooperation with the United States, but the Bush administration was not interested. . . .[9]

As thanks for Iran's efforts in aiding the fight on terror, President Bush used the occasion of his first State of the Union address in January 2002 to declare Iran a member of the "axis of evil"—along with North Korea and Iraq (a longtime enemy of both Iran but also al-Qaeda as well). Bush also refused to restore diplomatic relations, and instead aligned closer to Saudi Arabia, a longtime enemy of Iran and a country which has gone out of its way to aid the terrorists the United States is claiming to fight.

Bush's "axis of evil" speech emboldened hard-liners in Iran and weakened those who wanted a more cooperative relationship with the United States. As Iranian scholar Trita Parsi relates, "There are few examples where such an undiplomatic statement was made at such a sensitive time—just weeks after Iran had proved itself an indispensable ally in Afghanistan. Hard-liners in Tehran . . . argued that Iran shouldn't have offered the United States help without exacting a price up front." [10]

As Parsi explains, some of the Iranian diplomats who had been reaching out to the United States to find common cause in the war on terror and other areas of mutual concern "were later forced to pay for this fiasco with their careers, making others in Iran's foreign policy circles think twice before extending a hand of friendship to" the United States. Bush's clear message to Iran was, as the old adage goes, "no good deed goes unpunished."

President Bush's tough rhetoric against Iran, moreover, was combined with action, with the United States aggressively supporting terrorist attacks against that country while also imposing harsh economic sanctions. As journalist Jonathan Cook notes, beginning in 2005, the United States began supporting

a Pakistani militant group, led by a former Taliban fighter, that was launching guerilla raids into Baluchi areas of Iran. The group was kidnapping and murdering Iranians, as well as exploding bombs, in what appeared to be attempts at destabilizing the region. In addition to these repeated humiliations, the concerted attempts by the US and Israel to denigrate Iran's leader, the constant drumbeat of war against Tehran and the UN-imposed sanctions regime were pushing in the same direction: the weakening of social ties holding Iran together. [11]

All of this combined not only to embolden those in the Iranian leadership who wanted a tougher stance against the United States and adversaries in the region, but also helped to stymie the liberal reforms which had been taking place since 1997.

As Trita Parsi explains,

Iran had what some consider a second revolution on May 23, 1997. Defying Tehran's political and religious establishment, the Iranian people used what little room they had to send a clear signal to the

ruling regime: Change must come! Turning out in massive numbers,
they went to the polls and elected an unknown librarian, Seyyed
Mohammad Khatami, as their next president. Khatami ran on a plat-
form of rule of law, democracy, improved relations with the outside
world, and an inclusive political system. Thanks to a record turnout
of women and youth, Khatami won a landslide victory over his conservative opponent. . . . Not only would efforts to moderate Iran's
internal and external policies continue [as they had begun under
Khatami's predecessor], but they would significantly intensify in
spite of tough resistance from conservative elements in the regime.[12]

But Bush's aggressions against Iran impeded this burgeoning reform
movement. As Jonathan Cook explains, "In a predictable response,
Iran's government increased its repressive policies, reversing" the
liberalization process begun under President Khatami and further
straining social cohesion.[13]

Ultimately, Bush's designation of Iran as an enemy state, combined
with multiple attacks against the Iranian government and population,
played an important role in the election of Mahmoud Ahmadinejad,
considered by the West to be a "hard-liner," in 2005. Ahmadinejad
would remain as Iranian President until 2013. Iranians turned to
Ahmadinejad, who was much more hostile to the United States and
Israel, in direct reaction to the aggressive US stance toward Iran. In
short, they chose security over more rights, as voters so often do.

The liberal reforms which the West claims it wants to see in Iran
were consequently put off for almost another decade. At the same time,
it must be said that, as I learned in Iran, while Ahmadinejad was not a
reformer in the liberal sense, he did do much to support the poor in
Iran and remains very popular with the poor to this day. This is but
one more attribute of Ahmadinejad which the United States finds
reprehensible.

* * *

On another note, the *Washington Post* reported in December 2001, just after the US invasion of Afghanistan, that it was fully expected that there would be a surge in Afghan poppy production as a consequence of the invasion and the ousting of the Taliban which had, despite all its other many faults, been effective in its efforts to nearly eradicate the crop.[14]

And, of course, as predicted, the poppy crop production has exploded since the US invasion over sixteen years ago and despite, or possibly because of, the United States' huge presence there. As the *Washington Post* reported in 2006 in an article entitled, "Afghanistan Opium Crop Sets Record,"

> Opium cultivation was outlawed during Taliban rule in the late 1990s and was nearly eliminated by 2001. After the overthrow of the Taliban government by U.S. forces in the fall of that year, the Bush administration said that keeping a lid on production was among its highest priorities. But corruption and alliances formed by Washington and the Afghan government with anti-Taliban tribal chieftains, some of whom are believed to be deeply involved in the trade, undercut the effort.[15]

Going on to explain that by 2006 Afghanistan was providing 90 percent of the world's heroine, the *Post* quoted Afghan President Hamid Karzai as saying, "Once we thought terrorism was Afghanistan's biggest enemy" but now "poppy, its cultivation and drugs are Afghanistan's major enemy."

What all of this demonstrates is the utter bankruptcy of US policy, not only toward Iran, but also toward the rest of the world, particularly in the Middle and Near East, and how that policy is also devastating for us at home where Trump has just declared opiate addiction a "national health emergency."

Meanwhile, in an interesting move, the Taliban, in February 2018, published an open letter to the American people in which it laid its

case for why the United States should leave Afghanistan after seventeen years of occupation, and one has to admit that they set forth a
quite compelling case:

> In 2001 when your ex-president George W. Bush ordered the invasion
> of Afghanistan, his justification for that felonious act was the elimi-
> nation the Islamic Emirate (Taliban) and Al-Qaeda.
>
> But despite continuing this bloody war for seventeen years
> and accepting huge casualties and financial losses, your current
> president Donald Trump—to continue the illegal 17 year old war in
> Afghanistan—acknowledged increased insecurity and emergence
> of multiple groups instead of the single unified Islamic Emirate
> (Taliban). . . .
>
> No matter what title or justification is presented by your undis-
> cerning authorities for the war in Afghanistan, the reality is that tens
> of thousands of helpless Afghans including women and children
> were martyred by your forces, hundreds of thousands were injured
> and thousands more were incarcerated in Guantanamo, Bagram and
> various other secret jails and treated in such a humiliating way that
> has not only brought shame upon humanity but is also a violation of
> all claims of American culture and civilization.
>
> In this lopsided war and as confirmed by your own military
> authorities, 3546 American and foreign soldiers have been killed,
> more than 20,000 American forces injured and tens of thousands
> more are suffering mentally but in reality the amount of your casual-
> ties is several times higher and is deliberately being concealed by
> your leaders. Similarly this war has cost you trillions of dollars thus
> making it one of the bloodiest, longest and costliest wars in the con-
> temporary history of your country.[16]

What have we gotten for this expenditure of blood and treasure, the
Taliban ask? Their answer, which seems quite correct: "insecurity,
chaos and 87% increase in narcotics. . . . You proclaim to be a

developed and civilized nation of the world. Is this the civilization, modernity and rule of law proclaimed by you in the world?"

Describing itself in much the same way that Iranians could describe their country, the Taliban describe Afghanistan as "a country which has maintained its independence throughout its several thousand year history. Even in the 19th and 20th century when most Muslim countries were occupied by the then European imperial powers, Afghanistan was the only country in the region to preserve its independence and despite an eighty year imperialistic endeavor, the British failed to make them accept occupation." Of course, the Soviets could not subdue Afghanistan, aptly known as the "graveyard of empires," either.

And, neither can the United States. As the Taliban explains, "Only this past September—in accordance with Trump's new strategy—American forces used all their new powers and carried out 751 air strikes. You should ask your Generals that despite using such force, have you retaken even a single inch of land from the Taliban or have they become even more powerful." Of course, we know that the Taliban has only become more powerful.

The American people need to hear these quite rational words of the Taliban and realize that we have lost in Afghanistan, if there was ever anything there to win, and that we need to end the occupation and accept the inevitable rule of the Taliban, whether we like it or not. At the same time, we should learn from the experience in Afghanistan what heartache we would face by invading its next-door neighbor, Iran—another sizable country which has maintained its identity and unified nationhood for many centuries.

12

THE UNITED STATES, SAUDI ARABIA, AND THE WAR ON YEMEN

THERE IS NO BETTER EXAMPLE OF the utter depravity of the United States' foreign policy in the Middle East than the war on Yemen. And, as per usual, the US State Department, along with its compliant press, have attempted to justify the crimes upon that country due to the claimed need to counter the actions of Iran.

The United States' backing of the ugly war on Yemen began under President Obama, whose UN ambassador at the time was, quite ironically it turns out, Samantha Power. The irony is that Samantha Power is famous for her Pulitzer-prize winning book, *A Problem from Hell*, which condemned the world's failure to stop genocide throughout the world. As UN ambassador, however, Power would become an apologist for the genocide which the United States was, and continues to be, aiding and abetting in Yemen.

According to the standard narrative that we are meant to believe, the Saudi-led coalition (consisting mostly of other Gulf States like the United Arab Emirates) is fighting "Iran-backed" Houthis who ended up ousting the government of Yemen, at the time backed by the Gulf

Cooperation Council (GCC), in 2014. The Houthis are further described as "proxies for Iran."

Of course, once we hear the term "Iran-backed" or "Iran proxies," we are then meant to be at best indifferent to what suffering is inflicted upon those forces so described. The desired impact of such loaded language is in essence to lull us back into our usual posture of not caring.

The truth is, however, that (1) it is unfair to reduce the Houthis to some type of pawns or proxies of Iran as we are led to believe; and (2) whatever relationship they may have with Iran could not possibly justify the mass slaughter of Yemeni civilians which is being carried out by the Saudi coalition with critical US/UK assistance.

First, as Christopher Davidson points out, two successive US ambassadors to Yemen have expressed criticism about claims that the Houthis are somehow an "instrument of Iran" in the latter's alleged quest to secure a "beachhead in the Arabian Peninsula." Davidson further notes that such claims are belied by the Houthis' alliance with the Sunni groups in Yemen as well as the fact that "many of the tribes in 'fiercely Sunni areas' of Yemen were understood to have welcomed their advances in 2015." Indeed,

> [a] recent Saudi defector and former head of air operations at an airbase near Dhahran has largely corroborated this view, arguing this was not about sectarianism but rather 'a war [by the Saudi coalition] against the Yemeni nation and against Yemen becoming independent.' As anthropologist and Yemen specialist Gabriele vom Bruck has similarly pointed out, the Houthis 'want Yemen to be independent, that is the key idea, they don't want to be controlled by Saudi or the Americans, and they certainly don't want to replace the Saudis with the Iranians.'[1]

Similarly, Yemeni Nobel Peace laureate Tawakkol Karman recently told *Reuters* that what the war on Yemen is about is the effort of Saudi Arabia and UAE to "to exercise an ugly occupation and greater influence," and that Saudi Arabia and the United Arab Emirates had "betrayed the Yemenis and sold them out" by using the coup of the Houthi militia as a pretext for their expansionist aims.[2] She also stated, "Saudi Arabia and the United Arab Emirates (UAE), monarchies where the state and ruling families are intertwined, seek to turn back the clock on political progress in Yemen and abroad." She accused these countries of viewing "the Arab Spring as their first enemy," and called upon them to end their occupation of Yemen immediately.

But again, as is true with most foreign policy issues, the facts do not matter, just the labels the US State Department decides to paint those facts with.

Moreover, at the same time we are led to believe that the Yemeni war is about fighting "Iran-backed" Houthis, we are rarely told that the Saudi monarchial and retrograde coalition, and their plan for regional expansion, is "US-backed" and "UK-backed"—a fact which is undeniably true. As longtime peace activist Kathy Kelly—who I proudly spent an evening with in Cook County jail after being arrested for peacefully singing politically-themed Christmas carols in Chicago's Water Tower Place to protest the war in El Salvador—explains,

> The Iranian government [House Speaker Paul] Ryan denounced does have allies in Yemen and may be smuggling weapons into Yemen, but no one has accused them of supplying the Houthi rebels with cluster bombs, laser-guided missiles and littoral (near-coastal) combat ships to blockade ports vital to famine relief. Iran does not provide in-air refueling for warplanes used in daily bombing runs over Yemen [as the U.S. does]. The U.S. has sold all of these to countries in the Saudi-led coalition which have, in turn, used these weapons to destroy Yemen's infrastructure as well as create chaos and exacerbate suffering among civilians in Yemen.[3]

By refusing to honestly discuss such facts, the American press has been complicit in allowing for massive crimes in Yemen to continue.

And yet, very serious observers had been accusing President Obama for some time of committing war crimes through his logistical assistance to the brutal Saudi air offensive against Yemen. As *Foreign Policy* noted back in October 2015,[4] the fact that the United States is supporting the Saudi coalition military offensive against Yemen—in the form of intelligence, logistics (including mid-air refueling of Saudi jets), and even cluster bombs—and "inflicting extreme hardship on civilians in one of the Mideast's poorest countries provides an awkward counterpoint to the Obama administration's stated commitment to stand up for the region's oppressed people." The same article noted that even some US lawmakers were concerned about the legal implications for the United States:

> The humanitarian crisis in Yemen has received too little attention, and it directly, or indirectly, implicates us," said Sen. Patrick Leahy (D-Vt.), who noted that the airstrikes may violate legislation he authored barring the United States from providing security assistance to countries responsible for gross human rights abuses. "The reports of civilian casualties from Saudi air attacks in densely populated areas compel us to ask if these operations, supported by the United States, violate" that law, Leahy told *Foreign Policy* in an emailed statement.[5]

In addition to the military support for the Saudi coalition operations, this same piece explains that the United States has also provided diplomatic cover at the United Nations. Thus, the US Mission to the UN Security Council, including Samantha Power herself, scuttled a proposal which merely would have asked all the key actors to cooperate with human rights investigations in Yemen and would have reminded them to abide by international humanitarian law norms and human rights law in the prosecution of the conflict. Even this was too much for the United States, which has been hell-bent on seeing that this war goes on without limit.

Even after such serious criticism was being leveled against his actions, Obama decided to double down support for the Saudi coalition offensive, approving the sale of $1.29 billion in smart bombs to Saudi Arabia—a sale which, among other things, was intended to replenish Saudi Arabia's arsenal in attacking Yemen.

For his part, President Trump entered into a historically massive arms deal with Saudi Arabia near the beginning of his term in the spring of 2017, and as the war continued unabated. As *The Independent* explained,

> Donald Trump has signed the largest arms deal in history with Saudi Arabia despite warnings he could be accused of being complicit in war crimes and after blaming Saudi Arabia himself for producing the terrorists behind 9/11.
>
> The President confirmed he had signed a weapons deal with the Saudis worth $109.7 billion, predicted to grow to a $380 billion Saudi investment within 10 years, during his first trip abroad since his Inauguration. [6]

Meanwhile, the human toll of this conflict is simply staggering. The war on Yemen could in fact be the worst humanitarian disaster since WWII. Indeed, in early 2018 *Al Jazeera* quoted UN humanitarian chief Mark Lowcock as saying that what we are witnessing in Yemen "looks like an apocalypse" and predicting that Yemen could become the worst humanitarian disaster in half a century, with millions on the verge of starvation; the largest cholera outbreak in modern history, with a million people afflicted so far; and with an epidemic of diphtheria which will "spread like wildfire." [7]

In terms of Yemenis starving as a result of the combination of the war and US/Saudi blockade, the numbers are monumental. As the UN Office for the Coordination of Human Affairs (OCHA) relates:

> After more than three years of escalating conflict, Yemeni people continue to bear the brunt of ongoing hostilities and severe economic

decline. An alarming 22.2 million people in Yemen need some kind of humanitarian or protection assistance, an estimated 17.8 million are food insecure—8.4 million people are severely food insecure and at risk of starvation—16 million lack access to safe water and sanitation, and 16.4 million lack access to adequate healthcare. Needs across the country have increased steadily, with 11.3 million who are in acute need—an increase of more than one million people in acute need of humanitarian assistance to survive.[8]

What is just as incredible as the disaster in Yemen itself is the near silence about this crisis, and the US role in it, in the media. And, while few would be surprised that President Trump is complicit in this affair, it was actually President Obama that helped get it rolling, and yet this has not stopped his liberal base from nearly deifying him. This despite the fact that the numbers who will surely die in Yemen will rival or exceed those killed in the worst years of Joseph Stalin.

The disconnect on this issue is quite revealing of the dynamics of US foreign policy and how it is viewed in the US press and in the US consciousness. Obviously, this demonstrates the stark double standard between how we view the "crimes of others" and our own crimes. But also, it shows that just the mere specter of Iran being involved on the other side of a conflict seems to allow the United States off the hook for anything it does in that conflict. This shows how powerful the vilification of Iran is, even in a case where the United States and its allies are doing the lion's share of the killing.

The reaction to the events in Yemen is also reflective of another important phenomenon as well—that is, the long-standing view of the United States that those we have decided to subjugate have no right to self-defense. Thus, current UN Ambassador Nikki Haley recently went before the United Nations to try to prove that Iran had provided the Houthi rebels with short-range missiles which, she and the Saudis claimed, were fired upon Saudi Arabia a whopping total of two times![9] Haley declared that "the fight against Iranian aggression is the world's fight. The US is acting today in the spirit of transparency and international cooperation that is necessary to defeat this threat."[10]

Even putting aside the fact that the "evidence" of the Iranian supplying of such missiles is at best equivocal, with some UN experts serious expressing doubts about this claim,[11] what if this allegation were true?

In the same *Guardian* article, the authors state the obvious—that is, that "the Saudi-led coalition leading the fight against the Houthis in Yemen, which has been supplied with weaponry by the US, the UK and other allies, has been accused of the indiscriminate killing of civilians through its aerial bombing campaign and by its blockade of rebel-controlled areas of the country." The truth is that the "war" in Yemen is really a one-sided assault by the Saudi Coalition, with the support of the United States and the United Kingdom, against the Yemeni people.

The fact is that morality, international law (including Article 51 of the UN Charter), and just plain common sense allow for Yemen to defend itself against this attack. And, armed forces in Yemen have every right to attack Saudi Arabia in order to engage in such self-defense, and to enlist the support of others, like Iran, to help them do so. Under Article 51, this would be known as the right of collective self-defense.

But, since the founding of our country, such self-defense is not permitted of those we designate as our enemies, even if, as is almost always the case, they are much weaker than ourselves. As Vietnam veteran and longtime peace activist Brian S. Willson has explained, "imperial US military principles" were set forth centuries ago with George Washington's orders of 1789 to Major General Sullivan to "lay waste to all [indigenous] settlements around . . . that the [native] country not be merely overrun but destroyed . . . You will not by any means listen to any overtures for peace before the total ruin of their settlements. . . . Our future security will be in their inability to injure us . . . and in the terror which the severity of the chastisement they receive will inspire in them."[12]

From this order, Willson and others, like author John Marciano, have gleaned a number of principles, including the "crime of self-defense." The United States may brutalize and attempt to decimate an entire nation or people, but those people are never allowed to fight back. Such fighting back is indeed cause for even more brutality on the part of the United States. We see this time and again, for example in the Vietnam War when the claim that the Vietnamese attacked two US military vessels (this claim turned out to be untrue) in the Gulf of Tonkin enraged US Congressional representatives who then voted overwhelmingly in response to fund the war efforts which, up till then, they had been reluctant to do.

Again, forget the fact that the allegations were not factually true. Even if they were, the idea that somehow the Vietnamese could not fight back as the United States was demolishing their country with aerial bombs, napalm, and Agent Orange seems preposterous. And yet, that was in fact the overwhelming opinion of our leaders. Indeed, it would have been completely justifiable for Vietnam to attack the continental United States in order to defend itself (which of course never happened) but this seems unthinkable. Surely, the United States would have wiped it off the map if it had dared to do such a thing.

Similarly, I remember quite vividly, when, at the outset of the US invasion of Iraq in 2003, the two spokespeople for the Defense Department described in horror how the badly outgunned Iraqis were using guerilla tactics to try in vain to repel the invasion. One example given was how a pregnant Iraqi woman lured a US convoy into halting, whereupon she threw a grenade in its direction. The Defense spokespeople declared, without any tongue in cheek or any irony in their voice, that such tactics were actually proof of why the invasion was necessary to begin with. Surely, the argument went, any people who would engage in such self-defense tactics deserved to be attacked.

And, in the case of the Yemenis, if they dare try to defend them-selves from complete annihilation, and even go so far as to obtain help from our enemies, such as Iran, to do so, this is cause to punish the Yemenis and the Iranians even more. While such reasoning appears insane to the dispassionate observer, I cannot remember the last time someone called it out as such. This is so because the insane has become the new normal in the United States, especially when it comes to its treatment of others.

13

AVOIDING A WAR
WITH IRAN

Our swollen budgets constantly have been misrepresented to
the public. Our government has kept us in a perpetual state of fear—
kept us in a perpetual stampede of patriotic fervor—with the cry of a
grave national emergency. Always there has been some terrible evil at
home or some monstrous foreign power that was going to gobble us up
if we did not blindly rally behind it by furnishing the exorbitant funds
demanded. Yet, in retrospect, these disasters seem never to have
happened, seem never to have been quite real.
—General Douglas MacArthur, July 30, 1957

To SUM UP THE FOREGOING, THE United States ousted Mossadegh and
put in place the Shah who then, among other things, crushed the Iranian left with US encouragement and assistance. The people of Iran
rose up, quite predictably, against the murderous Shah, led first and
foremost by the only force left to lead them—the radical Islamic clerics.
Meanwhile, the United States supported the Mujahideen to undermine the secular, left government in Afghanistan, eventually ushering
in the Taliban and giving rise to al-Qaeda. Al-Qaeda then turned on
the United States and, among other things, carried out the atrocious

9/11 attacks against the United States. The United States, which had
been supporting the Taliban, then attacked the Taliban with the help
of Iran, but refused Iran's offer of an olive branch. As a consequence of
the Afghan invasion, meanwhile, the United States unleashed a huge
explosion in heroin production which continues to haunt our own citizens to this day.

The United States would then go on to attack Iraq after 9/11,
though it had nothing to do with 9/11, based upon claims about weapons of mass destruction which Iraq really didn't have. The United
States successfully overthrew Saddam Hussein, a mortal enemy of
Al-Qaeda, ushering in a Shiite government which, quite predictably,
aligned with Iran, thereby strengthening Iran's hand in the Middle
East. Now, the United States feels the need to weaken Iran given that
it had predictably strengthened Iran through the Iraqi invasion, and
the United States is aiding and abetting the very forces who attacked
us on 9/11 to carry out the containment of Iran.

And, instead of taking any responsibility for any of this, the United
States blames Iran, and to some extent Russia and Assad in Syria, for
all the problems confronting the Middle East, and the US government
would have us believe that one more regime change in Iran will help
fix all of this. Of course, this ignores the fact that none of the other
regime changes the United States has been involved in have done anything but make matters worse. And this should not be surprising given
the reactionary forces the United States has partnered with to bring
about regime change.

In his brilliant *Humanitarian Imperialism*,[1] the Belgian physicist
and intellectual, Jean Bricmont, explains that US imperialism can
indeed be distinguished from more traditional forms of colonialism in
that the latter, while certainly brutal and inexcusable, nonetheless
were modernizing to a degree in terms of spreading progressive medical ideas, advanced scientific knowledge, and liberal, democratic
values. The United States' imperial policy, on the other hand, "has
very often been directed against movements that were essentially

'modernizing' . . . and merely sought to enable those societies to bene-fit from the advantages of science, and, in some cases, democracy." And, "to defeat such progressive movements, Western powers have often supported the most feudal and obscurantist tendencies. . . ."

Sometimes, and indeed most times in recent years, the United States, when overturning a foreign government which has dared to stray too far beyond the reservation, does not even bother to replace it with any government at all. Take the case of Libya, for example, which is now ruled by chaos, and where there are now public slave markets, where human beings are auctioned off for as little as $400 a person, thanks to the NATO invasion of 2011.[2]

As one commentator correctly notes, the literally hundreds of thousands of bombs dropped on the countries of the Middle and Near East and Northern Africa by George W. Bush, Obama, and Trump, and the nearly 300,000 occupation troops these presidents have sent to 138 countries, "far from establishing the 'Pax Americana,' promised by policymakers and military strategists in the 1990s, from Paul Wol-fowitz, Dick Cheney to Madeleine Albright and Hillary Clinton, the results have been consistently catastrophic, producing what the new National Defense Strategy calls, 'increased global disorder, character-ized by decline in the long-standing rules-based international order.' "[3]

This same commentator quotes a US veteran of the Iraq and Afghan wars, and a former West Point instructor, Major Danny Sjursen, as candidly admitting, "The truth is, . . . I fought for next to nothing, for a country that, in recent conflicts, has made the world a deadlier, chaotic place."

In addition, this commentator opines that there are those in both political parties opposed to the Joint Comprehensive Plan of Action (also known as the "Iran Nuclear Deal"), despite the fact that Iran's compliance with the Plan has been well-documented, because of the dangerous precedent it sets—that negotiations between nations, treat-ing each other as equals, can actually succeed over war, one-side military intervention, and *coup d'état*, the latter being tactics which will always favor the militarily superior United States. This is a lesson which many in the US political and military establishment do not want other countries, like North Korea or Venezuela, for example, to learn.

Anyone looking at this series of events would have to conclude that the US intervention in the Middle and Near East, apart from destroying the lives of millions in that region, has been utterly counterproductive to the United States national security interests, at least if one views the safety of US civilians as synonymous with national security, and counterproductive to the United States' stated goals of advancing democracy and freedom.

Rather, the only interests which could possibly be viewed as being advanced by such an otherwise insane foreign policy are the oil companies and the military-industrial complex which profit from this policy—whether or not that policy succeeds in ways in which most rational humans would measure as success.

Meanwhile, the chances for a military conflict with Iran seem to be growing every day, and there are certainly officials in the White House who are gunning for such a war. At the same time, the American press appears to be doing its level best to fan the flames of war with an incessant refrain of blaming Iran for everything going wrong in the Middle East.

I am not the only one fearful of the United States' seeming plunge toward war with Iran, or of the dire consequences which would follow. Lawrence Wilkerson, who as chief of staff for Secretary of State Colin Powell wrote Powell's infamous UN "yellow cake" speech about Saddam Hussein's alleged pursuit of nuclear weapons—a speech which was so critical in paving the way for the invasion of Iraq in 2003—is also fearful.

Indeed, Wilkerson wrote an op-ed for the *New York Times* on February 5, 2018, in which he expressed this fear. This opinion piece is entitled, "I Helped Sell the False Choice of War Once. It is Happening Again."

In this piece, Wilkerson expresses his opinion, which is quite hard to dispute, that the 2003 invasion of Iraq "destabilized the entire Middle East." As he warns, "This should not be forgotten, since the Trump administration is using much the same playbook to create a false impression that war is the only way to address the threats posed by Iran."[4] Just as with the false claims about WMDs in Iraq that were the pretext for the 2003 invasion, Wilkerson notes that UN Ambassador Nikki Haley is now making false claims about Iran's ballistic missile program and about its role in Yemen, using the same game plan as the one used by Bush and Cheney back in 2003 to push us into a war with Iran now.

Wilkerson says that other obvious signs of a push for war with Iran can be seen in "the president's decertification ultimatum in January that Congress must 'fix' the Iran nuclear deal, despite the reality of Iran's compliance; the White House's pressure on the intelligence community to cook up evidence of Iran's noncompliance; and the administration's choosing to view the recent protests in Iran as the beginning of regime change."

He is not alone in this view. Thus, according to a research report published by the Congressional Research Service and authored by Kenneth Katzman, a former CIA analyst specializing in Iran, Iraq, and the Gulf states, Trump's putting Iran "on notice" that he may not recertify the Iran nuclear deal is strong evidence that he may be considering the possibility of pushing for regime change, including through military means.[5]

Moreover, Trump's recent appointments are a signal that war with Iran may be near at hand. The fact that Trump has appointed John Bolton, a longtime advocate of regime change in Iran and an open supporter of the MEK terrorists, as his national security adviser could be no greater evidence of Trump's violent designs upon Iran.

In addition, Trump has now nominated former CIA Director Mike Pompeo to replace Rex Tillerson as secretary of state—another ominous sign that we are drawing closer to war with Iran. As an initial matter, the very idea that a former CIA director with absolutely no diplomatic experience would head up the United States' diplomatic department should be frightening to anyone wanting a more peaceful world. Such a move suggests that the United States has given up on any desire to try to resolve its issues with other countries through discussion rather than confrontation and intrigue. Indeed, former CIA Director Pompeo as secretary of state will greatly resemble the Dulles brothers' simultaneous heading up of both the CIA and Department of State—a poisonous combination which led the United States into its fateful role in overthrowing Mohammed Mossadegh in Iran and Jacobo Arbenz in Guatemala.

Even more to the point, as *The Times of Israel* emphasizes, Pompeo is an avowed hawk on Iran, having "sought a more aggressive approach toward Tehran since joining the administration as CIA Director in January of 2017."[6] Pompeo has been opposed to the nuclear deal with Iran from the very beginning, and has taken every opportunity to vilify Iran, referring to it as "the world's largest state sponsor of terrorism," "a thuggish police state and a despotic theocracy." Incredibly, he has even equated the Islamic Republic of Iran with its mortal enemy ISIS.

According to Diplomacy Words, a group which has supported the Iran nuclear deal and which desires a more constructive relationship with Iran, Pompeo is an individual "who prefers military intervention over diplomacy," and whose elevation to secretary of state could "plunge our nation into another war in the region." Meanwhile, Saudi Arabia's crown prince, Mohammed bin Salman, expressed to CBS's *60 Minutes* that Saudi Arabia would be interested in developing its own nuclear weapons with the assistance of the West should the nuclear deal with Iran be scrapped and Iran decide to pursue a nuclear weapons program. The risk of some type of conflagration in the Middle East, with Iran at its epicenter, is indeed becoming a very real possibility.

For his part, Wilkerson rightly warns that a "war with Iran, a country of almost 80 million people whose vast strategic depth and difficult terrain make it a far greater challenge than Iraq, would be 10 to 15 times worse than the Iraq war in terms of casualties and costs," and would only further destabilize the Middle East. To put this more precisely, this would translate into a total of ten to fifteen million deaths and amount to $20 to $30 trillion in costs!

And, just as I do, Wilkerson laments the fact that "the American people have apparently become so accustomed to executive warmongering" that neither they, nor the mainstream press, are willing to contest "the politicization of intelligence and shortsighted policy decisions to make the case for war." Indeed, he is rightly appalled that "news outlets latched onto claims" about "Iran's [alleged] support of al-Qaeda's war with the United States," when in fact Iran has been a mortal enemy of al-Qaeda, and while US ally Saudi Arabia can more truthfully be said to be a friend to al-Qaeda.

Of course, this should not be surprising given the press' complicit role in pushing the lies that led us into the war with Iraq in 2003, and in pushing the lies and half-truths that have led us into every war we have fought since WWII.

In a separate interview with the *The Real News Network*, dated February 6, 2018, Wilkerson also makes it clear that, despite Israel's histrionic claims to the contrary, Iran does not pose a real threat to Israel.[7] The fact that Israel has about two hundred nuclear weapons to Iran's none is a good place to start in analyzing claims around this issue.

And finally, in the same interview, Wilkerson, quite interestingly, agrees with the assessment of Noam Chomsky that one of the big reasons that hawks in the US government are so bent on taking on Iran is because of what they see as the United States' humiliating loss to Iran in the 1979 overthrow of the US-backed Shah. As Chomsky himself put it, Washington is compelled by its perceived "need to punish Iran for overthrowing the murderous tyrant, the shah, imposed in 1953 by the US and UK coup that destroyed the Iranian parliamentary system." In the same way, the United States continues to punish Nicaragua for its 1979 revolution as well.

The standoff with Iran is becoming more dangerous every day. As I write these words, the news is reporting on a drone, which Israeli Prime Minister Benjamin Netanyahu claimed to be Iranian, being launched into the Golan Heights—a disputed area which was once a part of Syria (Syria still claims, it of course) and then seized by Israel in 1981, though the international community does not recognize this annexation. Netanyahu claimed that the "Iranian drone" was launched into Israeli territory—not technically true—and accused Iran, and Syria as well, of playing a very provocative and dangerous game with Israel. Netanyahu, meanwhile, has never been bashful about his desire to be rid of the current Iranian government.

CONCLUSION

AND SO, WHEREIN LIES THE PATH forward with Iran? In my view, the first place to start is to recognize Iran as a sovereign nation with the same rights as any country, including the United States, to exist and to exercise the type of government its people wish. Indeed, no less is guaranteed to Iran by the United Nations Charter which treats all nations as equal.

Another place to begin is to accept the fact that it is the United States which has caused immensely more suffering to Iran than they have or even could cause to us. Indeed, the average Iranian reasonably must wonder why the United States hates them so, having undermined and then overthrown their beloved prime minister in 1953; installed the Shah and helped create his repressive SAVAK; supported a brutal eight-year war against it, complete with banned chemical weapons attacks; shot down one of its civilian airliners; and continued to punish the people of Iran with Draconian economic sanctions, an oil war, and support of anti-Iranian terrorist groups.

In a very real way, the United States has, through decades of meddling, helped make Iran what it is today. Acknowledging this makes it much harder, of course, to vilify Iran and its government, for that government is a reflection of our interference in that country. The recognition of this also leads to the conclusion that there is no quick fix to Iran's problems, especially in the way of another Western-backed coup.

Self-described feminist and Iranian-American author Fathemeh Keshavarz, who wrote a book to try to counter the utterly negative picture of Iran painted by the wildly popular *Reading Lolita in Tehran* (*RLT*), warns against looking at Iran's current situation "with no reference to serious problems that plagued Iran under the Shah" and with the 1979 revolution made to appear as being "motivated by a longing for fanaticism and a dislike for freedom and modernization."[1] As Fathemeh explains,

> What is happening in the non-Western parts of the world, and in this case Iran, is a result of decades, at times centuries, of unresolved issues. While many local problems are at the root of these issues, the part that powerful nations of the world have played in sustaining—and at times exploiting—the mess is by no means negligible. These range from the outright colonization of territories and reckless pursuit of short-term economic goals to cultural illiteracy and disrespect. The resulting injustice, poverty, and totalitarianism are now exploding in our faces. The worst approach we can take to these problems is to consider them the work of the wicked witch, to be vanished with one move of the good fairy's magic wand.

Fathemeh, who lived under both the Shah and the Ayatollah, is critical of the one-sided portrayal of Iran by Azar Nafisi, the author of *RLT*, who lived only under the post-1979 revolutionary government and therefore lacked Fathemeh's more historical perspective.

As a side note, it is curious that Azar Nafisi received nearly $700,000 in US foundation grants before and just after publishing her book, which objectively served the interests of anti-Iranian hawks by absolutely trashing present-day Iran.[2] Of course, as the title suggests, the book is about the alleged intolerance of Iranian society, for example toward Western literature such as Vladimir Nabokov's *Lolita*.

As Fathemeh explains, Western literature is widely taught and read in Iran, including in the universities, and Azar Nafisi's dissertation on Nabokov was indeed published by Iran's Islamic government. Meanwhile, the choice of *Lolita* seems an odd one today in light of the #metoo movement which may look a bit askance at that novel about a middle-aged professor, the protagonist of the story, who drives a woman ("the cow" he calls her) to her death and then adopts and has a sexual relationship with her fourteen-year-old daughter. Many in the United States may now find some common ground with the Ayatollah about that book.

In any case, as Fathemeh correctly states, "the views portrayed in *RLT* may, in effect, prepare the American public for a tough line against Iran," with the violence, misogyny, and hating by some sectors of Iranian society presented, not "as an aberration, but rather as endemic to the local culture, making a harsh move against the culture seemed justified, perhaps even necessary."

Think if you will if one's view of the United States were reduced to its worst elements, including its frequent mass shootings; its glaring racial, gender, and economic inequality; its police shootings of unarmed civilians; its mass incarceration; its own misogyny and objectification of women, etc. Most Americans would cry foul at such a portrayal of the United States, but it is only such a portrayal of Iran that most Americans have ever known. And that, of course, is intentional because it primes Americans to support regime change and/or war against Iran.

In the end, we must acknowledge the reality, reinforced from history, that it is up to the Iranian people to determine their own fate and the nature of their own government. The idea that the United States can, or should even try, to force a change in government through coercive means such as sanctions, internal meddling, or war has been disproven time and again.

As Jean Bricmont emphasizes, "It is hard to believe that the situation would not have been better had Third World countries been

allowed to pursue their own ways of developing instead of being sub-
jected to leaders imposed by the West." As Bricmont urges, "Compare,
in terms of intelligence, humanity, and honesty, the leaders 'they' pro-
duced and those that the West supported against them: Arbenz and
the Guatemalan dictators, Sukarno and Suharto, Lumumba and
Mobutu, the Sandinistas and Somoza, Goulart and the Brazilian generals, Allende and Pinochet, Mandela and apartheid, Mossadegh and
the Shah, and today, Chavez and the Venezuelan putschists."[3]

Not surprisingly, the most prominent opposition groups and
reformists in Iran agree that it is up to the Iranian people, and them
alone, to chart their own course toward development. These same
groups and leaders are categorically against regime change efforts by
the United States.

For example, the outlawed and underground *Tudeh* Party, while
very critical of the Islamic government (not too surprisingly given
its brutal repression at its hands), is very clear that it is against foreign intervention, particularly by the United States, and against the
attempts by the United States to use, if not even instigate, protests in
Iran for the purposes of regime change. As the *Tudeh* Party explained
in a December 29, 2017, statement:

> Under the critical conditions of the current dangerous regional ten-
> sions, the regional reaction—supported by the Trump administration
> in the US and the right-wing government of Netanyahu in Israel—is
> seeking to distinctly impact the developments in our country and to
> replace the current reactionary regime with another reactionary
> regime. The support of these forces . . . for the Iranian monar-
> chists and those political groups whose agenda is to cooperate with
> the most reactionary regimes of the region and to persuade the
> European states to impose sanctions on Iran's economy—thereby
> exacerbating the misery for the destitute and disadvantaged people
> of our country - and to encourage foreign states to interfere militarily

in Iran, leaves no room whatsoever for any optimism regarding the future designs of such "opposition". The progressive and freedom-loving forces of Iran must increase their presence in the protest movement of the masses - more than ever before. . . .[4]

Other Iranian dissidents agree with this position of protesting the bad policies of the Iranian government while opposing the attempts by foreign powers, most notably the United States, to manipulate these protests for their own ends or to impose sanctions upon the country which only serve to hurt the people while leading to more repression by the Iranian state.

As Noam Chomsky explains:

Those who have attended to the history of sanctions will not be sur-prised to learn that US sanctions are perceived by Iranians as harmful to their cause. One of Iran's most influential intellectuals, Saeed Hajjarian, warns that 'America is looking for an excuse—the nuclear issue, terrorism, human rights, the Middle East peace process' to impose pressures on Iran, which often 'make the situation more mil-itarized, and in such an atmosphere democracy is killed.'" . . . He remains an opponent of sanctions, which 'hurt the people,' he says, and undermine democracy and freedom. . . .[5]

Indeed, Chomsky has opined, quite reasonably, that the very purpose of Western sanctions and coercive measures against Iran is "to pro-voke the Iranian leadership to adopt more repressive policies. Such policies could foment internal disorder, perhaps weakening Iran enough so that the United States might hazard military action."

Recall, for example, how the United States, in addition to waging punishing economic warfare against the Mossadegh government in the early 1950s, organized and paid unruly mobs in Iran to provoke Mossadegh into adopting repressive measures by the police which were then used as the very justification for the military to overthrow him. This was a tried and true game plan for regime change, but it is also a game plan which is greatly resented by Iranians to this very day.

In the end, the view of bona fide Iranian reform leaders, and the view which I believe is the most defensible one from a moral and legal point of view, is that it is up to the Iranian people themselves to make political change—and not up to foreign governments, with their own motives and agenda, to do so for them.

Putting it another way, as one of my Iranian communist friends told me when I was in Iran, "I would rather be killed by the Mullahs than by US soldiers." I note that the Iraqi Communist Party, which had supported the 2003 US intervention to topple Saddam Hussein— another violent anti-communist who the United States aided in wiping out his leftist opposition—now greatly regrets this position given the destruction and chaos left in the wake of the US invasion.

In the end, then, it is up to the Iranian people to make social and political change as they see fit. And, the chances of bringing about such change in Iran is more likely if the government is not pressured by sanctions, internal meddling, and other provocative acts which will only bring more suffering and more government repression upon the Iranian people.

Moreover, the truth is that, if the United States ever had legitimate interests in the Middle East and Persian Gulf to protect by force, it has much less so now given the fact that the main resource of this region— oil—is (1) quite plentiful, with the United States now producing more fossil fuels than any country in the world; and (2) less desirous given the need to fight global climate change by turning to alternative sources of energy.

But of course, as Noam Chomsky has pointed out, it has never been so much about access to oil, which we always have had, as it has been about controlling the world's energy supplies so that the United States and its energy industry could thereby control the world and maximize profit. Indeed, the recently-released CIA documents about the 1953 coup are replete with discussion about how the United States and United Kingdom really didn't need Iran's oil, and therefore could live without it while waiting for Mossadegh to fall. Then, the United States and Britain divided up Iran's oil in the interest of corporate profit, not in the interest of supplying themselves with oil which they could always get elsewhere.

In short, any rationale for the Carter Doctrine, if it ever truly existed, does not exist now. This should therefore allow the United States to relinquish control over the Middle East and the Persian Gulf and to allow countries like Iran to exist as they wish.

Meanwhile, the alleged military threat Iran poses to the United States and its partner Israel are greatly overblown, if not utterly nonexistent. The recognition of this reality should also allow the possibility of détente with Iran.

Thus, while both President Trump and Prime Minister Netanyahu claim the sky is falling because of Iran's nuclear program, there is simply no evidence to back this up. Thus, in 2003 and then again in 2007, the UN's International Atomic Energy Agency concluded that Iran did not intend to build a nuclear weapon, and this was confirmed by sixteen US intelligence agencies which collectively issued a Nuclear Intelligence Estimate stating, "with high confidence" that, if Iran ever had a nuclear weapons program, it halted such a program in the fall of 2003.[6]

As already stated in this book, moreover, the current Supreme Leader of Iran, Ayatollah Ali Khamenei, has indeed issued a Fatwah against the production, stockpiling, and use of nuclear weapons as inimical to the Islamic faith.

And of course, as authors like Stephen Kinzer, Robert Fisk, and Noam Chomsky have noted, to the extent the Islamic Republic of Iran has had the ability in the first place to enrich uranium, it has been because of the help of the United States dating back to Eisenhower which actively encouraged Iran's nuclear energy program. The Islamic Republic of Iran has always claimed that its nuclear enrichment program has been solely for energy purposes, and there seems to be no reason to doubt this. In any case, Israel, the only nuclear armed state in the Middle East, has nothing to fear from a nuclear Iran, and it knows this.

Another reason rapprochement with Iran is possible is that Iran desperately wants it. Indeed, even since the Islamic Revolution of 1979, and despite the legacy of cruelty inflicted by the United States upon Iran since 1953, Iran has shown a willingness to work with the United States, including, most notably, in fighting Islamist terrorism in the Middle East. And, on more than one occasion, Iran has taken the opportunity upon such occasions of cooperation to offer the olive branch to the United States.

For example, according to a PBS Frontline Report, shortly after the invasion of Iraq in March 2003 (and just as the Iranians had done just after 9/11) the Iranian reform president, Seyyed Mohammad Khatami, sent a fax to George W. Bush offering a "grand bargain," in essence a peace treaty between the United States and Iran, which put everything on the table, including Iran's alleged support for terrorism, its nuclear program, even its hostilities toward Israel. In exchange, Iran asked Washington for security guarantees, a lifting of sanctions, and a promise never to push for regime change.[7]

Incredibly, this olive branch had been presented by Iran even despite Bush's "axis of evil" speech in January 2002, and despite the United States' open support for terrorists to topple the Iranian government. Sadly, this fax was never even replied to.

Flynt Leverett, a former career CIA analyst and National Security Council director for the Middle East at the time, believes that the silence with which the United States responded to Iran's offer of a grand bargain was a huge missed opportunity, and he believes that the United States must open discussions for such a deal just as President Nixon opened the door to China.[8]

As Middle East expert Vali Nasr explains, "Iran is an indispensable component of any sustainable order in the Middle East."[9] And the

United States, which itself smashed the stability of the Middle East by its 2003 invasion of Iraq, must now reverse course, and "rely more on diplomacy and less on force," beginning with a diplomatic outreach to Iran and a brokering of peace between Iran and its rivals such as Saudi Arabia. One can only hope that there are still those in Washington who believe in such diplomacy over war.

In any case, given the terrible consequences of not reaching out to Iran in search of diplomatic solutions to the Middle East's problems, including a war which seems to be looming ever more each day, it seems that this is certainly worth a shot.

It is long overdue for the United States to reconsider President Eisenhower's query back in 1953, when he asked whether there is anything America could do to endear itself to the people of the Middle East. Regime change, massive bombings, and war have certainly not worked to improve the quality of life for people of that region or for the people of the West. It is high time that the United States withdraw militarily from the Middle East, and put its ample resources toward providing bread to the people there, rather than guns.

NOTES

Introduction

1   Phil Wilayto, *In Defense of Iran* (Richmond: Defender's Publications, 2008), pp. 42–43.

2   *Ibid.*, p. 44.

3   *Ibid.*, p. 124.

4   *Ibid.*, p. 124.

5   *Ibid.*, pp. 44, 64; and Shermin Kruse, "The Islamic Republic of Iran's Flavored Condoms, Free Vasectomies, and Gender Reassignment Surgery," *Huffington Post*, https://www.huffingtonpost.com/shermin-kruse/the-islamic-republic-of-i_2_b_5481323.html.

6   *Ibid.*

7   *Ibid.*

8   UNESCO World Heritage List, http://whc.unesco.org/en/list/115.

9   Wilayto, *In Defense of Iran.*

10   "Jewish Life in Iran Was Always Better Than in Europe," *Deutche Welle*, May 15, 2017.

11   Jonathan Cook, *Israel and the Clash of Civilisations: Iraq, Iran and the Plan to Remake the Middle East* (London: Pluto Press, 2007), pp. 51–52.

12   Documents from The US Espionage Den-Internet Archive, Vol 13(5), https://ia600205.us.archive.org/25/items/DocumentsFromTheU.s.EspionageDen/v13_5_text.pdf.

13   Tritia Parsi, *Treacherous Alliance, The Secret Dealings of Israel, Iran and the U.S.* (New Haven & London: Yale University, 2007), p. 6.

14   *Ibid.*

15   *Ibid.*

16   Jane Arraf, "Months After Isis, Much of Iraq's Mosul is Still Rubble," *NPR*, March 3, 2018, https://www.npr.org/sections/parallels/2018/03 /03/587726649/months-after-isis-much-of-iraqs-mosul-is-still-rubble.

17   *Ibid.*

18   Jeffrey St. Claire, "They Came, They Saw, They Tweeted," *Counterpunch*, Feb. 23, 2018, https://www.counterpunch.org/2018/02/23/99972/.

19   Javed Ali, "Chemical Weapons and the Iran-Iraq War: A Case Study in Noncompliance," *The Nonproliferation Review* (Spring, 2001).

20   Robert Fisk, *The Great War for Civilisation* (New York: Vintage Press 2005), pp. 211–212.

Chapter 1

1   General Wesley Clark interview with Amy Goodman, *Democracy Now* (2007).

2   Cook, *Israel and the Clash of Civilisations*, citing Seymour Hersh, "The Grey Zone," *New Yorker*, May 24, 2004, and "The General's Report," *New Yorker*, June 25, 2007.

3   *Ibid.*

4   Cook citing Martin Van Creveld, "Sharon on the Warpath: Is Israel planning to attack Iran?" *International Herald Tribune,* Aug. 1, 2004.

5   Cartalucci, Tony, "The Iran 'Nuclear Deal' Leads to War, Not Peace," *New Eastern Outlook,* Sept. 24, 2017.

6   Cartalucci citing Brookings Institute, "Which Path to Persia? Options For a New American Strategy Toward Iran," June 20, 2009, https://www .brookings.edu/wp-content/uploads/2016/06/06_iran_strategy.pdf.

7   Lakshmi Gandhi, "The History Behind The Phrase, 'Don't Be An Indian Giver,'" *National Public Radio*, Sept. 2, 2013.

Chapter 2

1   Cook, *Israel and the Clash of Civilisations*, p. 92.

2   Cook, *Israel and the Clash of Civilisations*, p. 84.

3   Stephen Kinzer, *All the Shah's Men* (Hoboken: John Wiley & Sons, Inc., 2008), p. 18.

4   George H. W. Bush, "Address Before a Joint Session of the Congress on the State of the Union," January 29, 1991, http://www.presidency.ucsb.edu/ws/?pid=19253.

5   Stephen Gowans, *Patriots, Traitors and Empires, The Story of Korea's Struggle For Freedom* (Montreal: Baraka Books, 2018) (citations omitted), pp. 42–43.

6   Parsi, *Treacherous Alliance*, p. xv.

7   *Ibid.*, p. xvi.

8   Sharmine Narwani, "How American Media Spin-Doctored the Iranian Protests," *American Conservative,* Feb. 18, 2018.

9   Bulent Gokay, "In Saudia Arabia's quest to debilitate the Iranian economy, they destroyed Venezuela," *The Independent*, August 9, 2017.

10 Vijay Prashad, "What the Protests in Iran Are Really About," *AlterNet* January 3, 2018.

11 Parsi, *Treacherous Alliance*, p. 245.

12 *Ibid.*, p. 246.

13 Tony Caratlucci, "American-Killing Terror Cult: U.S. Delists Mujahadeen e-Khalq (MEK)," *Global Research*, Sep. 22, 2012.

14 *Ibid.*

15 Tim Johnson and David Goldstein, "Accused in '70's of U.S. Military Slayings, Iran group has friends in Trump's Circle," *McClatchy News* Nov. 17, 2016.

16 Tony Cartalucci, "Iran: Lifting Sanctions and Coming Betrayal," *New Eastern Outlook*, Jan. 24, 2016.

17 Daniel Larison, "Bolton and the MEK," *The American Conservative,* March 27, 2015.

18 Johnson and Goldstein, *McClatchy News.*

19 *Ibid.*

20   Lawrence Wilkerson, "I Helped Sell The False Choice of War Once. It's
     Happening Again," *New York Times*, Feb. 5, 2018.

21   Seymour M. Hersh, "The Redirection: Is the Administration's new
     policy benefitting our enemies in the war on terrorism?" *New Yorker*,
     March 5, 2007, https://www.newyorker.com/magazine/2007/03/05
     /the-redirection.

22   Ben Norton, "US Ambassador Confirms Billions Spent on Regime
     Change in Libya, Debunking 'Obama Did Nothing' Myth," *The Real
     News Network*, Feb. 9, 2018.

23   "'Moderate Rebels' Are Actually Backed by ISIS & Al-Qaeda, Former
     US Ambassador Admits," *Mint Press News*, Feb. 3, 2016.

24   April 8, 2011, email from Sydney Blumenthal to Hillary Clinton,
     "Re: UK game playing; new rebel strategists; Egypt moves in," https://
     wikileaks.org/clinton-emails/emailid/12650.

25   Sam Jones, "Terrorism: Libya's civil war comes home to Manchester,"
     Financial Times, May 26, 2017.

26   Paul R. Pillar, "A New Decision to Go to War in Syria," *Global Research,*
     Jan. 25, 2018.

27   John Watling, "The Shia Militias of Iraq," *The Atlantic,* Dec. 22, 2016.

28   "15 Years Of War In Iraq, A Legacy John Bolton Has Yet To Reckon
     With," *NPR*, March 25, 2018, https://www.npr.org/2018/03/25/596805309
     /15-years-of-war-in-iraq-a-legacy-john-bolton-has-yet-to-reckon-with.

29   DIA Memo 12-L-0552/DIA/287, Judicial Watch, http://www.judicialwatch
     .org/wp-content/uploads/2015/05/Pg.-291-Pgs.-287-293-JW-v-DOD-and
     -State-14-812-DOD-Release-2015-04-10-final-version11.pdf.

30   Brad Hoff, "Former DIA Chief Michael Flynn Says Rise of Islamic
     State was 'a willful decision' and Defends Accuracy of 2012 Memo,"
     Levant Report, August 6, 2015, https://levantreport.com/tag/judicial
     -watch-dia-foia-release/.

31   Kate Brennan, "Obama: Forget About 'Destroying' ISIS, We just need to
     'Contain' Them," *The Daily Beast*, November 13, 2015.

32   Shebab Khan, "Henry Kissinger warns destroying Isis could lead to 'Ira-
     nian radical empire,'" *The Independent*, Aug. 7, 2017.

33   *Ibid.*

34   Vali Nasr, "Iran Among the Ruins," *Foreign Affairs*, Feb. 13, 2018.

35 Patrick Cockburn, "The massacre of Mosul: 40,000 feared dead in battle to take back city from Isis as scale of civilian casualties revealed," *The Independent*, July 19, 2017.

36 "At Any Cost: The Civilian Catastrophe In West Mosul, Iraq," Amnesty International 2017, https://www.amnesty.org/en/latest/campaigns/2017 /07/at-any-cost-civilian-catastrophe-in-west-mosul-iraq/.

37 Thomas Gibbons-Neff, "The airstrike in Mosul was potentially one of the worst U.S.-led civilian bombings in 25 years," *Washington Post*, March 28, 2017.

38 Andrew Curry, "Here Are the Ancient Sites ISIS Has Damaged and Destroyed," *National Geographic*, Sept. 1, 2015.

39 Noam Chomsky, *Failed States: The Abuse of Power and the Assault on Democracy* (New York: Henry Holt and Company, LLC, 2006).

40 Ayelett Shani, "Gaza Kids Live in Hell: A Psychologist Tells of Rampant Sexual Abuse, Drugs and Despair," *Haaretz*, Nov. 11, 2017.

41 Chomsky, *Failed States.*

42 Joy Bernard, "Amazon Removes Controversial Bestseller About Palestinian History," *Jerusalem Post*, June 28, 2017.

43 Gardiner Harris and Steven Erlanger, "U.S. Will Withdraw From UNESCO, Citing Its 'Anti-Israeli Bias,'" *New York Times*, Oct. 12, 2017.

44 Nasr, "Iran Among The Ruins."

45 Patrick Cockburn, *The Rise of The Islamic State: ISIS and the New Sunni Revolution* (London: Verso, 2015).

Chapter 3

1 "Iran, 1951-1954," Department of State, Office of the Historian, Bureau of Public Affairs (2017) (hereinafter, "2017 CIA Release"), https://history .state.gov/historicaldocuments/frus1951-54Iran.

2 Christopher Davidson, *Shadow Wars: The Secret Struggle for the Middle East* (London: One World Publications, Ltd., 2017), p. 60.

3 Wilayto, *In Defense of Iran*, p. 26.

4 Kinzer, *All the Shah's Men*, p. 39.

5 Wilayto, *In Defense of Iran*, p. 28.

6   Davidson, *Shadow Wars*, p. 52.

7   "Despatch From the Station in Iran to the Chief of the Near East and Africa Division, Directorate of Plans, Central Intelligence Agency (Roosevelt), November 13, 1953," contained in the 2017 CIA Release, p. 833., https://history.state.gov/historicaldocuments/frus1951-54Iran/d346.

8   Fleming, D. F., *The Cold War and Its Origins, 1917–1950*, Volume I (Garden City: Doubleday & Company, 1961), p. 341.

9   Wilayto, *In Defense of Iran*, p. 28.

10   Brian Wheeler, "The 'Iranian Schindler' who saved Jews from the Nazis," *BBC News*, March 8, 2012.

11   *Ibid.*

12   *Ibid.*

13   *Ibid.*

14   Marc Parry, "Uncovering the Brutal Truth About the British Empire," *The Guardian*, Aug. 18, 2016.

15   *Ibid.*

16   Mark Pilisuk and Jennifer Achord Rountree, *The Hidden Structure of Violence* (New York: Monthly Review Press, 2015), p. 192.

17   Kinzer, *All the Shah's Men*, pp. 151–152.

18   *Ibid.*, p. 144.

19   *Ibid.*, p. 152, (citing C. M. Woodhouse, *Something Ventured* (London: Granada, 1982)).

20   "April 16, 1953, Memo from Chief of Iran Branch, Near East and Africa Division (Waller) to the Chief of the Near East Africa Division, Directorate of Plans, Central Intelligence Agency (Roosevelt)," 2017 CIA Release, p. 527, https://history.state.gov/historicaldocuments/frus1951-54Iran/d192.

21   Wendy Lower, "Willkommen" (a review of *Operation Paperclip* by Annie Jacobsen) *New York Times*, Feb. 28, 2014.

22   Stephen Gowans, *Patriots, Traitors and Empires: The Story of Korea's Fight for Freedom* (Montreal: Baraka Books, 2018), pp. 30–31.

23   *Ibid.*

24   2017 CIA Release, p. 526, https://history.state.gov/historicaldocuments/frus1951-54Iran/d192.

25 2017 CIA Release, pp. 656–662, https://history.state.gov /historicaldocuments/frus1951-54Iran/d259.

26 *Ibid.*

27 *Ibid.*

28 2017 CIA Release. p. 539, "Information Report Prepared in The Central Intelligence Agency," April 17, 1953, https://history.state.gov /historicaldocuments/frus1951-54Iran/d193.

29 Kinzer, *All the Shah's Men*, p. 179.

30 2017 CIA Release, pp. 654–655, "Memorandum From Director of the U.S. Technical Cooperation Administration Mission in Iran (Warne) to the Charge d'Affaires in Iran (Mattison), August 6, 1953, https://history .state.gov/historicaldocuments/frus1951-54Iran/d258.

31 2017 CIA Release, p. 570, "Memorandum From the Director of the U.S. Technical Cooperation Administration Mission in Iran (Warne) to the Ambassador to Iran (Henderson)," https://history.state.gov /historicaldocuments/frus1951-54Iran/d207.

32 2017 CIA Release, p. 683, fn. 3, https://history.state.gov/historicaldocuments /frus1951-54Iran/d278.

33 2017 CIA Release, p. 481, "Memorandum of Discussion at the 135th Meeting of the National Security Council," March 4, 1953, https:// history.state.gov/historicaldocuments/frus1951-54Iran/d171.

34 *Id.* at p. 482.

Chapter 4

1 Kinzer, *All the Shah's Men*, p. 138.

2 2017 CIA Release, pp. 578–579, "Memorandum of Conversation," May 30, 1953, https://history.state.gov/historicaldocuments/frus1951-54Iran/d212.

3 *Ibid.*

4 *Ibid.*

5 2017 CIA Release, pp. 595–596, "Memorandum of Conversation," June 19, 1953, https://history.state.gov/historicaldocuments/frus1951-54Iran/d220.

6   2017 CIA Release, p. 634, "Paper Prepared in the Central Intelligence Agency," July 22, 1953, https://history.state.gov/historicaldocuments /frus1951-54Iran/d247.

7   2017 CIA Release, p. 546, "Telegram From the Embassy in Iran to the Department of State," May 4, 1953, https://history.state.gov /historicaldocuments/frus1951-54Iran/d199.

8   2017 CIA Release, pp. 595–596, "Memorandum of Conversation," June 19, 1953, https://history.state.gov/historicaldocuments/frus1951-54Iran/d220.

9   2017 CIA Release, pp. 567–568, "Memorandum From the Counselor of Embassy (Mattison) to the Ambassador of Iran (Henderson), May 19, 1953, https://history.state.gov/historicaldocuments/frus1951-54Iran/d206.

10   2017 CIA Release, p. 555, "Telegram From the Embassy in Iran to the Department of State," May 8, 1953, https://history.state.gov /historicaldocuments/frus1951-54Iran/d203.

11   2017 CIA Release, p. 612, "Despatch From the Embassy in Iran to the Department of State," July 1, 1953, https://history.state.gov /historicaldocuments/frus1951-54Iran/d233.

12   2017 CIA Release, p. 599, "Memorandum Prepared in the Bureau of Near Eastern, South Asian and African Affairs," https://history.state .gov/historicaldocuments/frus1951-54Iran/d223.

13   2017 CIA Release, p. 652, "Monthly Report Prepared in the Directorate of Plans, Central Intelligence Agency," July 1953, https://history.state .gov/historicaldocuments/frus1951-54Iran/d257.

14   2017 CIA Release, "Memorandum From the Chief of the Near East and Africa Division, Directorate of Plans, Central Intelligence Agency (Roosevelt) to Mitchell, July 8, 1953, https://history.state.gov /historicaldocuments/frus1951-54Iran/d236.

15   2017 CIA Release, "Memorandum From the Acting Chief of the Near East and Africa Division, Directorate of Plans, Central Intelligence Agency 9[name not declassified]) to Mitchell," July 22, 1953, https:// history.state.gov/historicaldocuments/frus1951-54Iran/d245.

16   2017 CIA Release, pp. 643–644, "Memorandum From the Chief of the Iran Branch, Near East and Africa Division, Directorate of Plans (Waller) to the Deputy Director of Plans, Central Intelligence Agency (Wisner),"

THE PLOT TO ATTACK IRAN 183

July 30, 1953, https://history.state.gov/historicaldocuments/frus1951 -54Iran/d255.

17 2017 CIA Release, p. 471, "Memorandum From Director of Central Intelligence Dulles to President Eisenhower," March 1, 1953, https://history .state.gov/historicaldocuments/frus1951-54Iran/d169.

18 2017 CIA Release, p. 757, fn. 5, "Despatch From the Embassy in Iran to the Department of State," September 11, 1953, https://history.state.gov /historicaldocuments/frus1951-54Iran/d316.

19 2017 CIA Release, p. 737, "Record of Meeting in the Central Intelligence Agency," August 28, 1953, https://history.state.gov/historicaldocuments /frus1951-54Iran/d307.

20 2017 CIA Release, p. 668, "Telegram From the Embassy in Iran to the Department of State," August 16, 1953, https://history.state.gov /historicaldocuments/frus1951-54Iran/d267.

21 Jefferson Morley, "The Gentlemanly Planner of Assassinations: The Nasty Career of CIA Director Richard Helms," *Slate*, Nov. 1, 2002.

22 "1953: MK-Ultra was hatched by Allen Dulles and Richard Helms," *Alliance for Human Research Protection*, http://ahrp.org/1953-mk-ultra -was-hatched-by-allen-dulles-and-richard-helms/.

23 *Ibid.*

24 Kim Zetter, "April 13, 1953: CIA Oks MK-Ultra Mind-Control Tests," *Wired*, April 13, 2010.

25 Richard M. Harley, "Chronology of Iranian Events Leading to Hostage Capture," *Christian Science Monitor*, Feb. 11, 1980.

26 2017 CIA Release, p. 645, "Memorandum From the Officer in Charge of Iranian Affairs, Office of Greek, Turkish, and Iranian Affairs (Stutesman) to the Director of the Office of Greek, Turkish, and Iranian Affairs, Bureau of Near Eastern, South Asian, and African Affairs (Richards)," Undated, https://history.state.gov/historicaldocuments/frus1951-54Iran /d256.

27 2017 CIA Release, p. 819, "Memorandum of Conversation," October 23, 1953, https://history.state.gov/historicaldocuments/frus1951-54Iran/d341.

28 *See, generally*, Bruce Cumings, *The Korean War: A History (Modern Library Chronicles)*, (New York: Modern Library, 2011).

29   Gowans, *Patriots, Traitors and Empires*, p. 73.

30   2017 CIA Release, pp. 472–474, "Memorandum Prepared in the Director-ate of Plans, Central Intelligence Agency," March 3, 1953, https://history.state.gov/historicaldocuments/frus1951-54Iran/d170.

31   2017 CIA Release, p. 536, "Memorandum From the Chief of the Iran Branch, Near East and Africa Division (Waller) to the Chief of the Near East and Africa Division, Directorate of Plans, Central Intelligence Agency (Roosevelt)," April 16, 1953, https://history.state.gov/historicaldocuments/frus1951-54Iran/d192.

32   2017 CIA Release, p. 503, "Progress Report to the National Security Council," March 20, 1953, https://history.state.gov/historicaldocuments/frus1951-54Iran/d180.

33   Wilayto, *In Defense of Iran*, p. 30.

34   2017 CIA Release, p. 631, "Memorandum From the Acting Chief of the Near East and Africa Division, Directorate of Plans, Central Intelligence Agency ([name not declassified]) to Mitchell," July 22, 1953, https://history.state.gov/historicaldocuments/frus1951-54Iran/d245.

35   2017 CIA Release, p. 680, "Memorandum Prepared in the Office of National Estimates, Central Intelligence Agency," August 17, 1953, https://history.state.gov/historicaldocuments/frus1951-54Iran/d275.

36   2017 CIA Release, p. 664, "Telegram From the Embassy in Iran to the Department of State," August 16, 1953, https://history.state.gov/historicaldocuments/frus1951-54Iran/d262.

37   2017 CIA Release, pp. 685–686, "Telegram From the Embassy in Iran to the Department of State," August 18, 1953, https://history.state.gov/historicaldocuments/frus1951-54Iran/d280.

38   2017 CIA Release, p. 699, "Telegram From the Station in Iran to the Central Intelligence Agency," August 19, 1953, https://history.state.gov/historicaldocuments/frus1951-54Iran/d286.

39   2017 CIA Release, p. 701, "Telegram From the Station in Iran to the Central Intelligence Agency," August 20, 1953, https://history.state.gov/historicaldocuments/frus1951-54Iran/d289.

40   2017 CIA Release, p. 729, "Record of Meeting in the Central Intelligence Agency," August 28, 1953, https://history.state.gov/historicaldocuments/frus1951-54Iran/d307.

41   2017 CIA Release, p. 740, "Monthly Report Prepared in the Directorate of Plans, Central Intelligence Agency," August, 1953, https://history .state.gov/historicaldocuments/frus1951-54Iran/d308.

42   2017 CIA Release, p. 761, "Briefing Notes Prepared in the Central Intelligence Agency for Director of Central Intelligence Agency Dulles," Undated, https://history.state.gov/historicaldocuments/frus1951-54Iran /d319.

43   2017 CIA Release, pp. 778–780, "Monthly Report Prepared in Directorate of Plans, Central Intelligence Agency," September, 1953, https://history .state.gov/historicaldocuments/frus1951-54Iran/d326.

44   2017 CIA Release, p. 815, "Memorandum of Conversation," October 23, 1953, https://history.state.gov/historicaldocuments/frus1951-54Iran/d341.

45   CIA 2017 Release, p. 810, "Memorandum From the Near East and Africa Division, Directorate of Plans to Director of Central Intelligence Dulles," October 29, 1953, https://history.state.gov/historicaldocuments/frus1951 -54Iran/d339.

46   2017 CIA Release, pp. 835–836, "Despatch From the Station in Iran to the Chief of the Near East and Africa Division, Directorate of Plans, Central Intelligence Agency (Roosevelt)," November 13, 1953, https://history .state.gov/historicaldocuments/frus1951-54Iran/d346.

47   2017 CIA Release, p. 927, "Editorial Note," https://history.state.gov /historicaldocuments/frus1951-54Iran/d372.

48   2017 CIA Release, p. 933, "National Intelligence Estimate," December 7, 1954, https://history.state.gov/historicaldocuments/frus1951-54Iran/d375.

49   Fisk, *The Great War for Civilisation*.

50   2017 CIA Release, pp. 826–827, "Despatch From the Embassy in Iran to the Department of State," November 5, 1953, https://history.state.gov /historicaldocuments/frus1951-54Iran/d344.

51   Andre Vltchek, *Western Terror From Potosi to Baghdad* (Mainstay Press, 2006), pp. 276–279.

52   *Ibid.*

53   Max Blumenthal, "The US is Arming and Assisting Neo-Nazis in Ukraine, While Congress Debate Prohibition," *The Real News Network*, Jan 19, 2018.

54   Kinzer, *All the Shah's Men*, p. 195.

55   2017 CIA Release, 950, Appendix, Summary of the Terms of the Oil
      Agreement between the International Oil Consortium and the Govern-
      ment of Iran, Signed 30 October 1954," https://history.state.gov
      /historicaldocuments/frus1951-54Iran/d375.

56   Kinzer, *All the Shah's Men*, pp. 201–202.

57   Kinzer, *All the Shah's Men*; and Fisk, *The Great War for Civilisation*.

58   2017 CIA Release, p. 781, "Editorial Note," https://history.state.gov
      /historicaldocuments/frus1951-54Iran/d328.

Chapter 5

1   Nafeez Ahmed, "U.S. State Department Spent over $1 million in Iran to
      Exploit Unrest," *Mint Press News*, January 29, 2018.

2   *Ibid.*

3   Dean Henderson, *Big Oil & Their Bankers in The Persian Gulf, Four Horse-
      men, Eight Families & Their Global Intelligence, Narcotics & Terror Network
      3rd Edition*, (Create Space, 2010).

4   Johnathan C. Randal, "SAVAK Jails Stark Reminder of Shah's Rul *Wash-
      ington Post*, December 13, 1979.

5   Fisk, *The Great War for Civilisation*, p. 99.

6   *Ibid.*, p. 99.

7   *Ibid.*, p. 112.

8   *Ibid.*, p. 99.

9   Memo from U.S. Embassy Tehran to US Secretary of State, April 28,
      1976, https://wikileaks.org/plusd/cables/1976TEHRAN04315_b.html.

10   A. J. Langguth, "Torture's Teachers," *New York Times*, June 11, 1979.

11   Memo from US State Department to US Embassy Tehran, March 7, 1975,
      https://wikileaks.org/plusd/cables/1975STATE051450_b.html.

12   Ryszard Kapuscinski, *Shah of Shahs* (New York: Vintage International
      Press, 1992), pp. 51–52.

13   Jonathan C. Randal, "SAVAK Jails Stark Reminder of Shah's Rule."

14   Kapuscinski, *Shah of Shahs*, p. 52.

15   Fisk, *The Great War for Civilisation*, p. 101.

16 Amnesty International Briefing: Iran, November 1, 1976, https://www
.amnesty.org/download/Documents/204000/mde130011976en.pdf.

17 *Ibid.*

18 *Ibid.*

19 Memo from US Dept. of State to US Embassy Tehran re: HIRC Hearings
on Human Rights in Iran, August 5, 1976, https://wikileaks.org/plusd
/cables/1976STATE193516_b.html.

20 Memo from US Embassy Tehran to US Department of State, March 19,
1973, https://wikileaks.org/plusd/cables/1973TEHRAN01726_b.html.

21 Amnesty International Briefing: Iran.

22 Amnesty International Briefing: Iran.

23 Amnesty International Briefing: Iran.

24 Amnesty International Briefing: Iran.

25 Memo from US Embassy Tehran to US State Department, December 5,
1978, https://wikileaks.org/plusd/cables/1978TEHRAN11882_d.html.

26 Amnesty International Briefing: Iran.

27 Memo from US Dept. of State to US Embassy Tehran re: HIRC Hearings
on Human Rights in Iran, August 5, 1976, https://wikileaks.org/plusd
/cables/1976STATE193516_b.html.

28 Davidson, *Shadow Wars*, p. 31.

Chapter 6

1 Nahal Toosi, "Leaked Memo Schooled Tillerson on Human Rights,"
Politico, Dec. 19, 2017.

2 Memo from Office of the Legal Adviser, Department of State to Secretary
of State, Re: Human Rights in Iran, March 6, 1975, https://wikileaks
.org/plusd/cables/1975TEHRAN02168_b.html.

3 Robert Parry, "A CIA Hand in An American Coup?" *Consortium News,*
August 26, 2013.

4 Jeff Cohen and Norman Solomon, "Jimmy Carter and Human Rights:
Behind the Media Myth," *Fairness & Accuracy in Reporting (FAIR)*,
September 21, 1994.

5   Letter can be found at the National Security Archive at George Washington University (Electronic Briefing Book No. 339), https://nsarchive2 .gwu.edu/NSAEBB/NSAEBB339/.

6   *Ibid.*

7   Noam Chomsky and Edward Herman, *Manufacturing Consent: The Political Economy of The Mass Media* (New York: Pantheon, 2002).

8   Mona Mahmood, et al., "From El Salvador to Iraq: Washington's Man behind brutal police squads," *The Guardian,* March 6, 2013.

Chapter 7

1   Fisk, *The Great War for Civilisation*, p. 127.

2   Documents from The US Espionage Den-Internet Archive, https:// archive.org/details/DocumentsFromTheU.s.EspionageDen.

3   Memo from US Embassy Tehran to US State Department, December 5, 1978, https://wikileaks.org/plusd/cables/1978TEHRAN11882_d.html.

4   Fisk, *The Great War for Civilisation*.

5   Documents from The US Espionage Den-Internet Archive, Vol 13(4), https://ia800205.us.archive.org/25/items/DocumentsFromTheU.s .EspionageDen/v13_4_text.pdf.

6   Documents from The US Espionage Den-Internet Archive, Vol 13(4), https://ia800205.us.archive.org/25/items/DocumentsFromTheU.s .EspionageDen/v13_4_text.pdf.

7   Documents from The US Espionage Den-Internet Archive, Vol 13(4), https://ia800205.us.archive.org/25/items/DocumentsFromTheU.s .EspionageDen/v13_4_text.pdf.

8   William Blum, "The Greek Tragedy: Some Things not to forget, which the new Greek leaders have not," *The Anti-Empire Report*, February 23, 2015.

9   *Ibid.*

10 Associated Press, "William Sullivan dies at 90; diplomat had key roles in Vietnam, Iran conflicts," *L.A. Times*, October 23, 2013.

11 Rich Whitney, "U.S. Provides Military Assistance to 73 Percent of World's Dictatorships," *Truthout*, Sept. 23, 2017.

12 Documents from The US Espionage Den-Internet Archive, Vol 13(4), https://ia800205.us.archive.org/25/items/DocumentsFromTheU.s .EspionageDen/v13_4_text.pdf.

13 *Ibid.*

14 *Ibid.*

15 *Ibid.*

16 *Ibid.*

17 *Ibid.*

18 Documents from The US Espionage Den-Internet Archive, Vol 13(5), https://ia600205.us.archive.org/25/items/DocumentsFromTheU.s .EspionageDen/v13_5_text.pdf.

19 *Ibid.*

20 *Ibid.*

21 *Ibid.*

22 *Ibid.*

23 Terence Smith, "Why Carter Admitted The Shah," *New York Times*, May 17, 1981.

24 Fisk, *The Great War for Civilisation.*

25 V. G. Kiernan, *America The New Imperialism, From White Settlement to World Hegemony* (London: Verso, 2005).

Chapter 8

1 Eqbal Ahmed, "The Iranian Hundred Years' War," *Mother Jones*, April 1979.

2 *Ibid.*

3 Davidson, *Shadow Wars*, pp. 16–19.

4 *Ibid.*

5 Hobsbawm, *The Age of Extremes*, p. 454.

6 Kapuscinski, *Shah of Shahs*, p. 58.

7 State Department Memo Re: Congressional Inquiry About GHOLAM-HOSSEIN SA'EDI (OR SAYEDI), Nov. 17, 1976, https://wikileaks.org /plusd/cables/1976STATE282142_b.html.

8 Fisk, *The Great War for Civilisation*, p. 98.

9 Kambiz Fattahi, "Two Weeks in January: America's secret engagement with Khomeini," *BBC*, June 3, 2016.

10 *Ibid.*

11 *Ibid.,* and Wilayto, *In Defense of Iran*, p. 53.

12 Malcolm Byrne and Mark Gasiorowski, "New Findings on Clerical Involvement in 1953 Coup in Iran," *National Security Archives at George Washington University*, Mar. 7, 2018.

13 Davidson, *Shadow Wars*, pp. 124–125.

14 Hobsbawm, *The Age of Extremes*, p. 455.

15 Vltchek, *Western Terror*, pp. 163–164.

16 Patrick Cockburn, "We finally know what Hillary Clinton knew all along—US allies Saudi Arabia and Qatar are finding Isis," *The Independent*, Oct. 14, 2016.

17 "Biden Blames US allies in Middle East for rise of ISIS," *RT News*, Oct. 3, 2014.

18 Simon Henderson, "What We Know About Saudi Arabia's Role in 9/11," *Foreign Policy*, July 18, 2016.

19 Paul Sperry, "Saudi government allegedly funded a 'dry run' for 9/11," *New York Post*, Sep. 9, 2017.

20 Cockburn, *The Rise of the Islamic State*, pp. xiv–xv.

21 The Brzezinski Interview with *Le Nouvel Observateur* (1998), translated from the French by William Blum and David N. Gibbs. This translation was published in Gibbs, "Afghanistan: The Soviet Invasion in Retrospect," *International Politics* 37, no. 2, 2000, pp. 241–242.

Chapter 9

1 Phaedra Hise, "How the Wright Brothers Blew It," *Forbes*, Nov. 19, 2003.

2 Gowans, *Patriots, Traitors & Empires*, pp. 51–52.

3 Noam Chomsky, *What Uncle Sam Really Wants* (Tucson: Odonian Press, 2002), p. 41.

4 Doyle McManus, "Rights Groups Accuse Contras: Atrocities in Nicaragua Against Civilians Charged," *Los Angeles Times* (March 8, 1985).

5   *Nicaragua v. United States (Case Concerning Military and Paramilitary Activities In And Against Nicaragua)*, International Court of Justice (June 27, 1986), http://www.icj-cij.org/files/case-related/70/070-19860627-JUD-01-00-EN.pdf.

6   *Ibid.*

7   *Ibid.*

8   *Ibid.*

9   Robert Parry, "Contras, Dirty Money and CIA," *Consortium News*, Dec. 19, 2013.

10   *Nicaragua v. United States.*

Chapter 10

1   Fisk, *The Great War for Civilisation*, p. 178.

2   *Ibid.*, p. 208.

3   *Ibid.*, p. 211.

4   *Ibid.*, pp. 211–212.

5   Ali, *"Chemical Weapons and the Iran-Iraq War: A Case Study in Noncompliance."*

6   *The Riegle Report: U.S. Chemical and Biological Warfare-Related Dual Use Exports to Iraq and their Possible Impact on the Health Consequences of the Gulf War*, May 25, 1994, http://gulfweb.org/bigdoc/report/riegle1.html.

7   *Ibid.*

8   Fisk, *The Great War for Civilisation*, p. 213.

9   Ali, "Chemical Weapons and the Iran-Iraq War: A Case Study in Noncompliance."

10   *Ibid.*

11   *Ibid.*

12   Gareth Porter, "When the Ayatollah Said No to Nukes," *Foreign Policy* October 16, 2014.

13   *Ibid.*

14   "The Iran-Contra Affair," *PBS.org.*

15   Trita Parsi, *Treacherous Alliance*, pp. 104–109; 112–113, and Peter Dale Scott, *The Iran-Contra Connection: Secret Teams and Covert Operations in the Reagan Era* (Boston: South End Press, 1987).

16   *Ibid.*

17   Davidson, *Shadow Wars*, pp. 514, 515.

18   Wilayto, *In Defense of Iran*, p. 22.

19   "The eight years' war between Iran and Iraq," *History.com.*

20   Nasr, "Iran Among The Ruins."

21   James C. Moore, "Not Fit to Print," *Salon.com*, Feb. 7, 2004.

22   Fisk, *The Great War for Civilisation,* p. 166.

23   Fisk, *The Great War for Civilisation,* p. 170.

24   "Chemical Weapons and the Iran-Iraq War: A Case Study in Noncompliance," Javed Ali, *The Nonproliferation Review* (Spring, 2001).

25   Eline Gordts, "Iraq War Anniversary: Birth Defects And Cancer Rates At Devastating High In Basra And Fallujah," *Huffington Post*, March 20, 2013.

26   Seymour Hersh, "The Red Line and The Rat Line," *London Review of Books*, April 17, 2014.

27   Rick Sterling, "When Is There Going to Be Accountability for US Wars and Aggression?" *Global Research*, Feb. 3, 2018.

28   "Colonel Lawrence Wilkerson: 'The Syrian chemical attack story is a hoax,'" *Intel Today* Aug. 10, 2017. gosint.wordpress.com.

Chapter 11

1   Geoff Earl, "How Trump was convinced to send more troops to Afghanistan—by top general showing him picture of women in 1970s Kabul in mini-skirts," *Daily Mail*, August 22, 2017.

2   Phillip Bonosky, *Afghanistan—Washington's Secret War* (New York: International Publishers, 2001), as quoted in *Censored 2003, The Top 25 Censored Stories*, Peter Phillips & Project Censored (Seven Stories Press, 2002), p. 153.

3   John J. Maresca, vice president of Unocal, in testimony before a U.S. House Committee, February 12, 1998, as cited in *Censored 2003, The Top*

25 Censored Stories, Peter Phillips & Project Censored (New York: Seven Stories Press, 2002), p. 150.

4   Ahmed Rashid, "U.S.-Taliban Relations–Friend Turns Fiend," as quoted in *Censored 2003, The Top 25 Censored Stories*, Peter Phillips & Project Censored (New York: Seven Stories Press, 2002), p. 150.

5   *Washington Post*, May 25, 2001, as quoted in Censored 2003, The Top 25 Censored Stories, Peter Phillips & Project Censored (New York: Seven Stories Press, 2002), p. 151.

6   Charles Brisard and Guillaume Dasquie, *Bin Laden, The Forbidden Truth*, as quoted in *Censored 2003, The Top 25 Censored Stories*, Peter Phillips & Project Censored (New York: Seven Stories Press, 2002), p. 152.

7   Bedi, Rahul, "India Joins Anti-Taliban Coalition," *Janes Defense Newsletter*, March 15, 2001, as quoted in Censored 2003, The Top 25 Censored Stories, Peter Phillips & Project Censored (New York: Seven Stories Press, 2002), p. 144.

8   David Ray, "Osama bin Laden Responsible for the 9/11 Attacks? Where is the Evidence?" *Veterans Today & Global Research*, Oct. 30, 2009.

9   "Iran Gave U.S. Help on Al Qaida After 9/11," *CBS/AP*, October 7, 2008.

10   Parsi, *Treacherous Alliance*, p. 235.

11   Cook, *Israel and the Clash of Civilisations*, p. 84.

12   Parsi, *Treacherous Alliance*, p. 202.

13   Cook, *Israel and the Clash of Civilisations*, p. 84.

14   Marc Kaufman, "Surge in Afghan Poppy Crop is Forecast," *The Washington Post*, December 25, 2001.

15   "Afghanistan Opium Crop Sets Record," Karen de Young, *Washington Post* (Dec. 2, 2006).

16   *Taliban Open Letter to The American People*, February, 2018, https://www.facebook.com/barnett.r.rubin/posts/10155295387646447.

Chapter 12

1   Davidson, *Shadow Wars*, p. 355.

2   "Saudi, UAE 'betrayed' Yemen, Nobel laureate says," *Middle East Monitor*, Feb. 8, 2018.

3   Kathy Kelly, "A Treacherous Crossing," *Consortium News*, Feb. 8, 2018.

4   Colum Lynch, "U.S. Support for Saudi Strikes in Yemen Raises War Crime Concerns," *Foreign Policy*, Oct. 15, 2015.

5   *Ibid.*

6   Rachel Revesz, "Donald Trump signs $110 billion arms deal with the nation he accused of masterminding 9/11," *The Independent*, May 21, 2017.

7   "Yemen could be 'worst' humanitarian crisis in 50 years," *Al Jazeera*, Jan. 5, 2018, https://www.aljazeera.com/news/2018/01/yemen-worst -humanitarian-crisis-50-years-180105190332474.html.

8   OCHA summary of crisis in Yemen, http://www.unocha.org/yemen /about-ocha-yemen.

9   Julian Borger and Patrick Wintour, "US gives evidence Iran supplied missiles that Yemen rebels fired at Saudi Arabia," *Guardian*, Dec. 14, 2017.

10 *Ibid.*

11 Colum Lynch and Robbie Gramer, "Haley's 'Smoking Gun' on Iran Met With Skepticism at U.N.," *Foreign Policy*, Dec. 14, 2017.

12 John Marciano, *The American War in Vietnam: Crime or Commemoration?* Monthly (New York: Monthly Review Press, 2016), p. 28.

Chapter 13

1   Jean Bricmont, *Humanitarian Imperialism* (New York: Monthly Review Press, 2006), p. 40.

2   Nima Elbagir and Raja Razek, "People for Sale, Where Lives are Auctioned for $400," Alex Platt and Bryony Jones, *CNN*, Nov. 15, 2017.

3   Nicolas, J. S. Davies, "Sowing Global Chaos as a National Defense Strategy," *Mint Press News*, Jan. 24, 2018.

4   Lawrence Wilkerson, "I Helped Sell the False Choice of War Once. It is Happening Again." *New York Times*, February 5, 2018, https://www .nytimes.com/2018/02/05/opinion/trump-iran-war.html.

5   Nafeez Ahmed, "U.S. State Department Spent over $1 million in Iran to Exploit Unrest," *Mint Press News*, January 29, 2018.

6   Eric Cortellessa, "In Mike Pompeo, Trump taps Iran hawk whose views dovetail with his own," *The Times of Israel*, March 13, 2018.

7   Aaron Mate, "Wilkerson: On Iran, Trump Follows the Iraq Playbook,"
     The Real News Network, Feb. 6, 2018, http://therealnews.com/t2/index
     .php?option=com_content&task=view&id=31&Itemid=74&jumival
     =21061.

Conclusion

1   Fatemeh Keshavarz, *Jasmine and Stars, Reading More than* Lolita *in
     Tehran* (The University of North Carolina Press, 2007), pp. 10–11.
2   Wilayto, *In Defense of Iran*, p. 140.
3   Bricmont, *Humanitarian Imperialism*, p. 39.
4   Tudeh Party of Iran, "Statement of the Tudeh Party of Iran on the popu-
     lar protest movement in the country," 29 December 2017, http://solidnet
     .org/iran-tudeh-party-of-iran/tudeh-party-of-iran-statement-of-the-tudeh
     -party-of-iran-on-the-popular-protest-movement-in-the-country-29
     -december-2017-en.
5   Noam Chomsky, *Failed States, The Abuse of Power and the Assault on Democ-
     racy* (New York: Henry Holt & Company, LLC, 2006), p. 63.
6   Wilayto, *In Defense of Iran*, p. 94.
7   *Ibid.*, p. 35.
8   "The 'Grand Bargain' Fax: A Missed Opportunity?" *PBS Frontline*.
9   Nasr, "Iran Among The Ruins."